To: Nancy

God [illegible]

MW01105386

With love,

Tessa

Don't Stop at the Gate

Living a Life of Childlike Faith

Tessa Gaines

Scripture taken from The Message. Copyright © 1993, 1994, 1995, 1996, 2000, 2001, 2002. Used by permission of NavPress Publishing Group.

Scripture quotations taken from the Amplified® Bible, Copyright © 1954, 1958, 1962, 1964, 1965, 1987 by The Lockman Foundation Used by permission." (www.Lockman.org)

Scripture taken from the New King James Version. Copyright © 1982 by Thomas Nelson, Inc. Used by permission. All rights reserved.

Scripture quotations taken from the New American Standard Bible®, Copyright © 1960, 1962, 1963, 1968, 1971, 1972, 1973, 1975, 1977, 1995 by The Lockman Foundation Used by permission. (www.Lockman.org)

Scripture quotations taken from THE HOLY BIBLE, NEW INTERNATIONAL VERSION®, NIV® Copyright © 1973, 1978, 1984, 2011 by Biblica, Inc.™ Used by permission. All rights reserved worldwide.

Scripture quotations marked KJV are taken from the King James Version of the Bible.

Italics in Scripture quotations have been inserted by the author for emphasis.

©2011 Tessa Gaines. All rights reserved.

No part of this book may be reproduced, stored in a retrieval system, or transmitted by any means without the written permission of the author.

Cover Photo by R. Gregg Marion
Illustrations by Ashley Gaines and Amber Lawson
Printed in the United States of America
This book is printed on acid-free paper.

Because of the dynamic nature of the Internet, any web addresses or links contained in this book may have changed since publication and may no longer be valid.

I dedicate this book to my loving husband. You have been an inspiration to me as I have witnessed you bravely face the challenges of aplastic anemia. I have watched God's amazing grace gloriously shine through you. You truly are a living example of childlike faith. I am so thankful to God for the love that we share and our wonderful friendship.

To my daughter—you are an amazing gift from God. You bring such joy to my life, and it is an honor and pleasure to be your mother.

And most importantly, I dedicate this book to my precious Lord. You have blessed my life beyond comprehension. Thank you for choosing me. May this work not only display but also promote your glory among the nations.

Contents

Foreword

One late summer afternoon while watering the flowers in my backyard, I couldn't help but notice our large wild cherry tree. The tree was thriving. Its leaves were green and lush, and its branches were overloaded with cherries.

What I found most admirable about the tree on this particular day was its appearance compared to years past. Several years before, my husband and I were convinced this tree wouldn't survive. It had dropped most of its leaves, and the few cherries hanging from its branches were withered. It was providing very little shade and seemed to be just getting by.

Imagine my enthusiasm that afternoon as I admired this vibrant tree and stood in the nice, cool shade it provided. We have many trees in our backyard, but this particular one is very special. This wild cherry tree is important because it has grown into the perfect position to provide shade on the deck at the back of our home where we enjoy sitting in the hot summer afternoons. This tree not only provides shade for my family but also for our animals—not to mention the food it provides for the birds living in the neighboring trees.

While I stood admiring the tree, I felt in my spirit that God was trying to get my attention. As I thought back a couple of years and was reminded of the appearance of the tree before, I began to wonder what had happened to make such a change. Why was it so healthy, strong, and productive, when just a couple of years ago, it appeared to be just getting by? I turned my focus to God and very quickly understood.

We had experienced several long seasons of rain, and the large amounts of rain had made the difference. The water was just what the tree had needed. The Lord began to show me that the tree was similar to our lives as believers. Sometimes in our lives, all we need are a few rainy seasons.

I began to look back, and I realized my life did somewhat resemble this tree. When I compared my life that day to the one I was living two years prior to my husband's illness, I was amazed at the difference. Although I thought at the time that I was very happy and living the life God had planned for me, I was living a stress-filled life consumed with worry and fear. All along the way, I believed that I had faith in God; I certainly proclaimed to trust Him. I was so deceived. I am sorry to say that my actions did not prove to anyone—especially God—that I trusted Him. God most certainly uses the rainy seasons in our lives to teach and grow us.

> "And the God of all grace, who called you to his eternal glory in Christ, after you have suffered a little while, will himself restore you and make you strong, firm and steadfast" (1 Peter 5:10, NIV).

Introduction

The day before my forty-fourth birthday, I found myself in a hospital room, sitting by my husband, Robert, waiting for test results. Fear consumed me as the doctor entered the room, and I anticipated his diagnosis. "You have aplastic anemia," the doctor announced as he stood somberly by my husband. He then began to explain the rare disease that only three in one million people were diagnosed with each year. My husband's immune system had become confused and was attacking his bone marrow.

That day was surreal—one I thought I would always want to forget. I had never even heard of this disease. My head was spinning. I never dreamed that after twenty-three years of marriage, my husband would be lying in a hospital, fighting for his life. He had always been so healthy and strong.

It is hard to explain what goes through one's mind at a time like this. *I have to be dreaming! That's it—I'm going to wake up any minute, and this will all go away.*

Growing Pains

One of my favorite pastimes is sharing how I see and experience God in my everyday life. Keep in mind that I am not a teacher or a pastor, but just an average person who watches and enjoys acknowledging and sharing God's handiwork. As I have walked beside my husband the last couple of years as he has battled aplastic anemia, God has taught me (and continues to teach me) so many things. Since Robert's illness, the Word of God has come alive in my life, and I hope and pray that maybe something I share with you will help you better relate God's Word to your life.

I want to start by asking a question: How do you think God feels about you? It sounds sort of like a trick question, doesn't it? I think the normal response for most believers would be to say, "I know that Jesus died for me, so yes, He loves me." Or maybe some might say, "I think that God is probably mad at me, because I have been doing some things that He doesn't approve of." Some might even say, "I know that God isn't happy with me, because I haven't done something I was supposed to do."

All of my life, I have heard about the love of God in the Bible, devotionals, and in many songs; but so often, I have had a hard time wrapping my mind around His love.

So first, I want to begin by reminding you that God loves you! I realize it is possible that you are thinking, "Goodness, I already know that. Why are you telling me something that I already know?" Well, I think the real question that I have for you is, "Do you *really* know and understand the love He has for you?"

Until recently, I felt I had a pretty clear understanding of the love God has for me. But even after all of the blessings God has poured on my family—especially in the last couple of years—I still didn't grasp the depth of His love. It wasn't until I experienced an unusual but very awesome encounter with the Lord that I came closer to completely understanding His love.

One Sunday morning at church, during the worship service, a sweet little baby in front of me caught my eye. This lovable little girl was in the arms of her mother. This baby was absolutely adorable. She kept looking at me and smiling as she checked out her surroundings. She was very happy and content in her mother's arms. I couldn't seem to take my eyes off her as I admired her precious face. Watching the mother and daughter made me think of my daughter when she was that age. I was reminded of the endless mercy and the pure, unconditional love that I feel as a parent—especially when I held my daughter in my arms when she was a baby. There isn't anything like the love one feels for a child. That love really is hard to put into words.

Near the end of the service, our pastor offered the congregation a time of prayer. As I closed my eyes and my focus turned to the Lord, I suddenly felt His presence in a really strong way. I felt an overwhelming sense that the feelings pouring out of my heart as I admired this sweet little baby were just a tiny example of how God feels about me. Just as this mother held her baby close, He also holds me very close to Him, and He absolutely adores me! I quickly responded to Him, "But God, how could you feel that way about me after all that I have done? This baby is so innocent and pure, and she has never done anything wrong. I am such a sinner, and I just don't understand how you could still love me that deeply." He then again brought to my attention the feelings I have for my daughter. I suddenly felt in my spirit that He wanted me to reflect on how I feel when my daughter does something I don't approve of. Do I love her any less? I immediately thought, "No, I love her unconditionally, and nothing could stop me from loving her with all of my heart."

If you have a child of your own, you probably better understand this love to which I am referring. But for those who do not have any children, take a moment and think of the cutest baby you have ever seen. When you think of watching that baby, pay attention to how you feel. This is just a taste of how your Father feels about you as He watches you! Doesn't the presence of a happy baby or small child bring a smile to your face? Isn't your heart flooded with mercy, admiration, patience, and understanding?

As I witnessed the mother caring for the baby girl, I noticed that the baby's tiny fingers held tightly to her mother's shirt. I was reminded that this is how our Lord wants us to live. He created us! He is our Father, and He wants us to hold tightly to Him.

God's love is hard to comprehend. He feels this way about all of His children, and I hope my experience will help you keep this mental picture and better understand just how much He loves you—like it did me.

In Luke 18:17, Jesus teaches us that He wants us to come to Him as a child. This is how the Father wants us to respond to Him. He wants us to hold tightly to Him, just like the baby girl held to her mother's shirt, and to look to Him to protect, care for, and love us.

You might ask, "How could you possibly say that God loves you that much? Look at what your family has been through the last couple of years. Your husband has a life-threatening illness, and you have no idea what will happen. Your future seems so uncertain." Well, I would have to agree that to the world, our lives are very uncertain. But with God leading the way, our lives couldn't be more certain! We simply trust Him and His promises.

Throughout the last several years, not only have ours lives been shaken up by this disease, but we have witnessed many of our family members and friends, without warning, suddenly find themselves in really bad circumstances. But I have learned that we should not allow ourselves to become alarmed when something bad happens. We should stay calm and remember that God is in control. Staying calm is a sign to God that we trust Him. Besides, sometimes things are not what they seem to be on the surface. Let me explain by sharing one of my journal entries from last year:

> As I was putting away the dishes from lunch today, I glanced through the window to the deck outside in the backyard. My attention was drawn to the grill as I became very aware that something was on the side of the lid. It appeared to be a dried, crumbled leaf that had fallen from the tree. I continued to place my dishes in the dishwasher, and several minutes later, I glanced out the window a second time. My attention was again drawn to the dried leaf on the lid of the grill—although this time, the leaf began to move. At second glance, I realized that what I had thought to be a leaf wasn't a leaf at all. As the object began to move, the wings of a butterfly appeared. I was gazing at a beautiful butterfly! As I admired its beauty, it suddenly took flight and flew away.
>
> In my spirit, I felt God was showing me that things we see on the surface—like challenging circumstances or even the bad actions of others—are not always as they seem. Under the surface of those ugly circumstances, there might just be something beautiful—like that butterfly. He has taught me that He wants us to face every challenge with an attitude of faith. He wants us to look at those challenges not as dried-up, dead leaves, but to search for the butterflies underneath the surface of those bad circumstances. The enemy wants us to only see the dead leaves. But through our relationship with God and relying on His strength and wisdom, we can find those butterflies, and we can allow God to use us to produce something beautiful and to influence people in a positive way.

As I have witnessed others going through tough times in the past few years, I have noticed something very interesting about their lives. The ones who look to God and hang on tightly to Him through their bad circumstances have lives that always seem to work out for good. It might not be comfortable for them for a season, and the outcome of their circumstances might not always turn out as they had hoped, but in the end, God turns things around for them. The Word tells us in Romans 8:28–29, "That's why we can be so sure that every detail in our lives of love for God is worked into something good. God knew what he was doing from the very beginning. He decided from the outset to shape the lives of those who love him along the same lines as the life of his Son" *(The Message).*

I want to encourage you, if you are going through something that you don't understand, no matter how big or small, to simply turn to the Lord. Hang on tight, trust Him, and in the end, He will work your circumstance into something good. In Hebrews 12:7, we are instructed to "Endure hardship as discipline; God is treating you as His children. For what children are not disciplined by their father?" (NIV)

In Hebrews 12:11, the Word says, "No discipline seems pleasant at the time, but painful. Later on, however, it produces a harvest of righteousness and peace for those who have been trained by it" (NIV). As stated in the words of Phillip Brooks in L. B. Cowman's *Streams in the Desert,* "Faith does not say, 'I see this is good for me; therefore God must have sent it.' Instead, faith declares, 'God sent it; therefore, it must be good for me.'"[1]

The past few years have been quite a challenge for my family, but God has been faithful and good to us. He has been there and helped us with every little detail. Once again, allow me to explain by sharing one of my journal entries:

> After Robert's diagnosis, I have made it a priority to not allow myself to spend much time (if any) thinking about how I feel about the changes that have occurred in our lives. On this particular morning, I was spending time with the Lord and trying to obtain some down time and rest, you might say, from the change and stress of our life with aplastic anemia. As I poured out my heart to Him, I took just a few minutes to feel the pain of what had taken place in our lives in the past year. It was very painful! I was feeling very drained and was just

> trying to adjust to the changes and the loss of how our lives used to be.
>
> After my time of prayer, I sat down at my computer to check my e-mail. Flashing at the top of the screen from an advertisement were the words "Growing Pains" in very large letters. They jumped off the page at me. The path that God leads us down can sometimes be very challenging and painful; but with every path or experience, God does a work in us. As we draw closer to Him through these experiences, we grow. God was showing me that what I was feeling were growing pains, and I was very comforted by Him. He knows how hard it can be, and just as we hold our children's hands through their growing pains, He holds ours and is always there to listen and comfort us. I know in my life He usually uses something tragic involving someone that is very dear to my heart to bring me to a higher level in my relationship with Him. It is almost always the very painful times in our lives that we learn the most about God.

God is our comforter and has done exactly what His Word promises us in Romans 8:28. He has taken our circumstances and worked them out for good. As we experience Him through every uncomfortable circumstance, His presence gives us the grace to endure, and each experience blesses us with newfound peace and trust. He also fills our lives with wonderful family and friends who He uses as His hands and feet to minister to us.

~

> "Faith, when walking through the dark with God, only asks Him to hold his hand more tightly" (L. B. Cowman, *Streams in the Desert)* [2]

~

Early after Robert's diagnosis, as we prepared for our hospital stay while Robert received his chemotherapy treatments, a very special friend gave me these verses. These are two of God's promises that truly comforted us. The first is from 2 Chronicles 20:15: "This is what the LORD says to you: 'Do not be afraid or discouraged because of this vast army. For the battle is not yours, but God's'" (NIV). 2 Chronicles 20:17 says, "You will not have to fight this battle. Take up your positions; stand firm and see the deliverance the LORD will give you. Do not be afraid; do not be discouraged. Go out to face them tomorrow, and the LORD will be with you" (NIV).

You see, aplastic anemia is really the biggest battle that we have ever had to fight. These words helped me understand that we don't have to fight this battle on our own strength, but that God is with us to fight for us! The Lord has shown me that if we focus on Him through every battle in our lives, He will always be present to fight for us. We just need to hang on to Him tightly and completely trust Him, and He will provide and care for us. He has been true to His Word.

> "The Lord will fight for you, and you shall hold your peace and remain at rest" (Exodus 14:14, AMP).

Don't Fall for It

My family and I recently watched the movie *Sherlock Holmes* starring Robert Downey, Jr. and Jude Law. As I watched *Sherlock Holmes,* I was intrigued by the parallels between this movie and what I had been led to write.

The story takes place in London in 1890, and Dr. Watson has declared a condemned man dead after his hanging. After being buried, the condemned man, Lord Blackwood, emerges days later from the tomb. Holmes and Watson solve the mystery of the emerged Lord Blackwood.

If you haven't seen this movie, I highly recommend it—but not for the reasons that you might think. As you enjoy the entertainment, notice the connotations in the plot. In my opinion, Lord Blackwood represents the devil and the dark forces of the universe. The story is built around an illusion that Lord Blackwood has risen from the dead, and the evil force controls a city of people through deceit and manipulation. The town is totally consumed by fear and left helpless against this force. The power this man possesses is actually given to him by the people through their fear. After the great detective solves the mystery, we are shown the deceptive strategy the enemy used to deceive the people of London. What they saw and heard was only an illusion, and their inability to see the truth left them powerless.

I believe that this storyline, although presented in the 1890s, is very similar to what is presently happening in today's society. The enemy creates illusions to intimidate and control our emotions, which in turn influences our actions.

The *American Heritage Dictionary* defines illusion as "an erroneous (mistaken or false) perception of reality, a misconception."[1] I think this definition is the perfect example of what the enemy does with our minds. He deceives us with a false perception of reality. Just like a magician convinces his audience to believe that his tricks are actually real, the enemy creates illusions almost everywhere we look to deceive us.

An example of this deception occurs when you turn on the evening news. As you watch the news, do you notice your mood changing after seeing all the bad reports? Would you say that you start to feel despair and become discouraged? There is usually more that takes place in our minds than just accepting the information made available to us. When our minds accept the bad news we have just heard, we most certainly do feel our moods change initially. In my experience, the enemy feeds off the bad news. It is at this time that our minds seem to be flooded with destructive thoughts along with the bad news.

Don't misunderstand me; I know that there are a lot of bad things going on in the world. We need to be informed and aware of these things, but this is just a good example of an illusion from the enemy that happens in my own life. In this case, the information that has just been reported is true and is information that we probably do need to know. I certainly don't believe in sticking your head in the sand and just denying that there are problems today. But this kind of information is exactly what the enemy uses to tempt us.

For example, after hearing about another school shooting, my mind immediately experiences very negative thoughts. Yes, it is normal to feel sad and sorry for the victims and the families involved—that's a healthy response. But the enemy doesn't waste any time bringing that incident home to me. The thought that a shooting could easily happen at my daughter's school is front and center. This thought leads to the thought that she isn't safe, which leads to another, and another—and before I realize it, I suddenly feel very fearful. I can easily become worried and quite discouraged.

In this example, I have just taken the bait and fallen into the trap or stepped into an illusion from the enemy. He wants me to believe that people in the world today are only doing bad things. At this point, I have lost my joy and peace. I am left feeling helpless and the enemy has succeeded.

If this scenario sounds all too familiar to you, then let me remind you that God is still in control! God is *alive,* and His Word is *true.* My family has taken God at His Word, we have stood on His promises, and He has been faithful! There are still many great people in the world doing a lot of wonderful things. The enemy sees the opportunity given by the negative stories, and attempts to frighten and persuade us to believe his illusions. I think I have believed and lived in the enemy's illusions my whole life—I just wasn't aware of it until recently.

In *Sherlock Holmes,* Lord Blackwood, who represents the evil force, uses his illusions to scare and gain power over the people. In reality, do you see that the enemy is no different in our lives? The devil is crafty! We can innocently be convinced that deceptive thoughts are true and easily be manipulated by fear.

Fear can be a very destructive and powerful force, and it has definitely captured my attention the last couple of years. Fear has been a very big challenge for my family as we walk through our lives with aplastic anemia.

From the very beginning, when we were introduced to this unfamiliar disease, we were also introduced to fears we had never encountered. These fears would have led to total destruction in our lives if it had not been for the Lord helping us understand and giving us wisdom. With this disease, the devil works overtime tempting us to worry and become fearful. The enemy is merciless, and he has an endless supply of ammunition.

I honestly think the emotion of fear is a very big barrier in all of our lives. God repeatedly commands us in His Word not to fear. Shouldn't that get our attention? With God, there is no need to be afraid. The Word tells us in 2 Timothy 1:7, "For God has not given us a spirit of fear, but of power and of love and of a sound mind" (NKJV). The Word also tells us in 1 John 4:18, "There is no fear in love, [dread does not exist], but full-grown, (complete, perfect) love turns fear out of doors and expels every trace of terror!" (AMP)

God's plan for His children was certainly not for them to be found helpless, powerless, and controlled by fear in any situation. In Isaiah 41:10, the Word tells us, "Do not fear, for I am with you; do not be dismayed, for I am your God. I will strengthen you and help you; I will uphold you with my righteous right hand" (NIV).

Over the past couple of years, God has given me a better understanding of the power that He has made available to us, and I think He wants us to learn how to execute His power in our lives.

"Now to Him who is able to do immeasurably more than all we ask or imagine, according to His power that is at work within us, to Him be the glory in the church and in Christ Jesus throughout all generations, for ever and ever!" (Ephesians 3:20–21, NIV)

~

We have established that fear is obviously not from God. I believe that fear is one of the enemy's favorite weapons! He uses it to debilitate his prey, which in turn gives him power. I honestly think that it is at our weakest times that the enemy is the most deceiving and is given the most power, and fear can render us helpless in these moments if it is not immediately recognized and challenged.

An example from my own journey illustrates how the enemy can strike when we are at our weakest. When Robert was staying in the hospital, receiving and then recovering from his chemotherapy treatments, I found myself alone in our home on many occasions. I became very familiar with just how powerful and intimidating the force of fear can be. I would become totally consumed by fear in the empty house. It was as if there were an evil spirit in the house, and it taunted me the entire time I was alone. As long as there was someone in the house with me, I was fine; but the minute I was left alone, this demonic spirit would attack me.

I recognized that this was a spiritual battle of some sort, and I turned to God and His Word to rescue me. I would speak God's Word out loud as I showered and dressed, and I would worship God, trying to focus only on Him. The frightening thoughts of what my life would be like at my home alone if Robert didn't survive flooded my mind. I felt that I was fighting for my life—fighting to keep my head above the water of these attacks. The enemy was trying to bring me down and intimidate me. These were truly some of the most difficult times that I remember going through during those first few months. I asked several people to pray for me during my alone time in the house.

Through God's Word, His grace, and good friends who prayed for me, God walked me through it. He even led one of my closest friends to my door on one particular morning when I seemed to be losing the battle. She had been walking, and she stopped by the house. She prayed with me, and when she left, I knew that God had brought her there to strengthen me.

When we are unaware of the conflicts that take place in our minds, we become great targets. We can easily be sabotaged by the enemy and bound by fear. We have to stay alert and make sure that we don't allow him to intimidate us.

We will always experience fearful moments throughout our lives. The important thing is what we do with the feeling of fear when it comes. Will we let it control and intimidate us?

We have to be very careful not to allow fear to keep us from God's best for our lives. To put it bluntly, we have to put more faith in God and His promises than we do in the enemy! When we allow fear to control us, we are putting more faith in the enemy than we are in God. This is the bottom line: Faith allows God the opportunity to move in our lives—but fear allows the enemy to move in our lives.

Before this experience with Robert, I honestly didn't realize how many different types of fear were controlling me. And, yes, as hard as it is to admit this, my actions were proof that I put more faith in my fear and the enemy than in God. God has shown me in many different ways how I have allowed the enemy to intimidate and keep me from experiencing the great life that He has planned for me.

For instance, like many people, I have always battled with the fear of public speaking. I was totally consumed by fear when I got up in front of my church one day to share my testimony with the congregation. I was absolutely terrified! This was the day that I felt God opening my eyes and helping me better understand what was taking place in my thought life.

Interestingly enough, as I drove home from church that day, I heard the following statement on the radio: "We fear the worst, and when the worst comes, it is not as bad as we feared it would be. And God is there, and He doesn't walk away."

This is so simple, and it makes so much sense to me. God is bigger than anything we fear. Why are we afraid of so many things? As I thought about getting up in front of the church to speak, the fear and anxiety were extreme. Why is it that we are so afraid to get up in front of a group of people—especially when we are in a building of believers? In my case, most of the congregation consisted of my family and friends. What is the worst thing that could happen? There's not much, when you really think about it. I can only imagine how God must feel when we know that He wants us to do something and we choose not to take action because we feel fear.

As a parent, I have tried very hard to teach my daughter life's many lessons. When she faces decisions in her life and has to make choices, if she chooses to not apply the lessons that I have instructed—even if it is because of fear—I would have a very difficult time understanding her actions. Her decision to disobey me or to not take my advice would be a sign to me that she really didn't trust me. This would be very hard to comprehend after all I have done to prove to her that I am trustworthy and that I only want what is best for her. Her decision would be proof that she doubted me.

Sadly, I have fallen into the trap of becoming fearful and choosing to be disobedient many times. As I look back at my life, I realize that fear has been my major obstacle, and it directly reflects in my disobedience. Although God knows my heart and has amazing mercy and patience with me, I can only imagine how frustrated He must get with me.

In my life, I have just not had the courage to step out of the boat and take chances. When Robert was diagnosed with aplastic anemia, I felt like we had been *thrown* out of the boat. It felt as if we had been thrown far, far from the boat. I couldn't even see the boat for a while! But I now know that I was thrown out into the arms of God.

God would never allow us to be placed into a situation or thrown out of the boat unless He was there to catch us. When I think about this, I am reminded of being by a pool and watching children learn to swim. Parents stand in the water and wait to catch their children as the children jump from the side into their parents' arms. The children usually have some type of flotation device on their arms or waists so they won't sink when they hit the water.

This is similar to how I feel about my life and what has happened to me personally. Although I didn't willingly jump into the deep water myself, when I hit the water, my Father was there to catch me, and God's Word was there to keep me afloat. Unfortunately, I would never have had the courage to get out into the deep on my own.

Only now have I become very comfortable being out of the boat and in the arms of God. I trust Him with everything, and I know beyond a shadow of a doubt that He wants what is best for me.

The Word teaches us in Nehemiah 8:10, "The joy of the Lord is your strength" (KJV). Jesus actually tells us in John 10:10, "The thief comes only in order to steal and kill and destroy. I came that they may have and enjoy life, and have it in abundance (to the full, till it overflows)" (AMP).

What the enemy is really after is our joy. If we allow him to steal our joy and peace, then we feel weak and vulnerable, and we become unproductive. In 1 Peter 5:8, the Word tells us to "be well balanced (temperate, sober of mind), be vigilant and cautious at all times; for that enemy of yours, the devil, roams around like a lion roaring [in fierce hunger], seeking someone to seize upon and devour" (AMP).

So many people are absolutely miserable and unhappy—and only because they are being deceived by the enemy and fall into this trap on a regular basis. In the past, I struggled with unhappiness. To be very frank, I believe that I was lulled into a comfortable relationship with bondage. I grew so comfortable with fear that I didn't know how to live without it.[2]

Fear remains a constant challenge, and I am still deceived on a regular basis. But as I spend more time in God's Word, I am continually reminded by the Holy Spirit that this act of deceit is taking place, and I am becoming more aware of the traps the enemy sets for me. So you see, "The Lord is my strength and my shield; my heart trusts in him, and he helps me" (Psalm 28:7, NIV).

God is omnipotent, and He has overcome the enemy's deceiving ways. How great is our God? He wants His children to be wise and understand that these traps are keeping us from carrying out His plans and holding us back from what He has created us to do!

One of my favorite books is *Experiencing God Day by Day* by Henry and Richard Blackaby. This daily devotional book is filled with such wonderful faith-builders that I would recommend it to anyone. I love this quote from the book:

> "What you do reveals what you believe. If you are living a fearful, anxiety-filled life, you are proving your lack of confidence in God's protection, regardless of what you may say. Live your life with confidence that Jesus is continually interceding with the Father on your behalf. If you trust Him completely, you will have nothing to fear."[3]

No One Is Good

Having a husband battling a life-threatening illness creates its challenges, but I have discovered that some of the greatest challenges for me as the spouse actually originate in my mind. Everyone faces challenges or battles in life, but I feel the Lord has shown me that a lot of my challenges are basically a reflection of my thoughts. I realize this is a very strong statement, so let me explain.

Everything that we say and do begins with our thought life. I have recently learned that we obviously can't always control our circumstances or the thoughts that go through our minds, but we can control how we respond to them. This has been something that I have struggled with all my life. Before our lives were totally disrupted by this disease, I couldn't grasp this concept completely. Our thoughts directly affect our actions and the choices that we make in life. I think that everyone struggles with this to some extent, and I believe that this is where the devil is the most productive.

As I have described the connection that I feel our contemporary lives have with *Sherlock Holmes,* I want to bring something to your attention once again. Did you notice that I mentioned earlier that the power that Lord Blackwood possesses is actually given to him by the townspeople through their fear?

One of the most important lessons God has taught me since Robert became ill is that the enemy doesn't have the power I once thought he had. In my opinion, his biggest advantage is his craftiness. He knows how to manipulate us, and he obtains his power through us. What do

I mean by this? To understand where I am going, let me cover a few points first.

There are typically two completely different types of thoughts going through our minds. A better explanation might be to say that we have two different voices in our heads. We have all seen the cartoons of the angel on a person's right shoulder and the devil on the left shoulder. I actually feel this is similar to what takes place in our thought lives. Our minds continually experience good and bad thoughts throughout each day.

Let me run a few questions by you. Do you believe that God forces Himself on anyone? Are we given the opportunity to choose between following God or the enemy? In a believer's life, could it be possible that listening and following God is as simple as recognizing and responding to the good thoughts in our minds instead of to the bad?

Let's back up a minute and discuss something before we continue. Years ago, I was in a Bible study with a small group from my church. Prepare yourself for what I am getting ready to say, because this is going to be quite hard to swallow. In this study, we learned that nothing good that we do originates from us, but that any good thing we do comes only from God! When I heard this, I was shocked. As I have studied recently, I stumbled over something else that blew me away!

In Luke 18:18-19 we are told that a rich young ruler approached Jesus one day and asked Him a question. Notice how Jesus responded: "'A ruler questioned Him, saying, 'Good Teacher, what shall I do to inherit eternal life?' And Jesus said to him, 'Why do you call Me good? No one is good except God alone'" (NASB).

Wow, does that blow you away? Take a minute to swallow that truth, and let's go back to where we left off.

We have established that the good thoughts are from God—so we would have to assume that the bad thoughts originate from the enemy, right? In order to better understand this concept, let's refer to the good thoughts as positive and the bad thoughts as negative, and then let's look at their definitions.

The *American Heritage Dictionary* defines positive as: "displaying affirmation, confident and real, not fictitious." It also defines positive used in photography as: "having the areas of light and dark in their original and normal relationship."[1]

How do we relate this to God? God's Spirit that lives inside us is real, not fictitious. If you will notice the definition as it pertains to photography, positive is having the areas of light and dark in their original and normal relationships. I realize this definition is related to photography, but I think it is also the perfect definition of what God and His Word do in our lives. When we allow God and His Word to direct us, everything is put into perspective, and God adorns our life. God's Word is positive! It is against God's nature to be negative.

The *American Heritage Dictionary* defines negative as: "lacking the quality of being positive or affirmative." It also defines negative as: "an image in which the light areas of the object rendered appear dark and the dark areas appear light."[2]

Notice that the definition says the light areas of the object appear dark, and the dark areas appear light. Would you say that negative thoughts might possibly allow your mind to see things differently than they really are? Quite deceptive, don't you think? Isn't that what the enemy does? Is it possible that negative thoughts deceive you? When negative thoughts or questions arise in your mind, aren't you immediately tempted to worry over them? If you give in to the temptation, before long, you find yourself stressed out over something that most often isn't even reality. You might find yourself getting angry at someone or having hurt feelings over something that never actually happened. You could even become very sad over something that may never happen, because you accept and believe those negative thoughts.

Recently a verse in God's Word concerning this subject got my attention. This verse is in John 13, and it pertains to the story of Judas betraying Jesus. We are actually told in this verse that Satan put the thought of betraying Jesus into the heart of Judas. I believe that this is an obvious example of the enemy using negative thoughts to influence someone: "So [it was] during supper, Satan having already put the thought of betraying Jesus in the heart of Judas Iscariot, Simon's son" (John 13:2, AMP).

You see, there is a battle going on in our minds. God's Word better explains this in Ephesians 6:11–12: "Put on the full armor of God so that you can take your stand against the devil's schemes. For our struggle is not against flesh and blood, but against the rulers, against the authorities, against the powers of this dark world and against the spiritual forces of evil in the heavenly realms" (NIV).

The Word also instructs to "gird up the loins of your mind" in 1 Peter 1:13 (NKJV).

Now that we better understand our thought life, let's go a little further. We obviously want positive thoughts going through our minds. In Philippians 4:8, the Word reminds us that we are to dwell on positive thoughts. "Finally, brothers and sisters, whatever is true, whatever is noble, whatever is right, whatever is pure, whatever is lovely, whatever is admirable—if anything is excellent or praiseworthy—think about such things" (NIV).

Negative thoughts can easily lead us in the wrong direction and get us off track. We can innocently be deceived if we allow ourselves to dwell on negative or deceptive thoughts. As our minds get caught up in these thoughts, all the enemy has to do is watch and wait, and *we* take care of the rest. How? We are persuaded to believe the thoughts or lies, and we immediately become controlled. This manipulative act of persuasion can not only steal our joy, but lead us into making bad choices which can often keep us from doing the will of God. We can easily become filled with fear, doubt, intimidation, and an array of other emotions which totally shut us down and keep us from stepping out and living the life that God has planned for us.

In John 8:44, Jesus describes the enemy as "the father of lies and of all that is false." He also explains in this verse that the enemy "does not stand in the truth, because there is no truth in him. When he speaks a falsehood, he speaks what is natural to him, for he is a liar [himself] and the father of lies and of all that is false" (AMP).

Do you see that the enemy really has no power to control our thoughts and attitudes unless we allow him? Do you see that his power is actually given to him through us? I truly believe that we hand this power over to him unconsciously.

We can't actually stop the negative thoughts which tempt us, but again, I will remind you that we *can* change how we react to them. The good news is the "God of Glory doesn't deceive and He doesn't dither.

He says what He means and means what He says" (1 Samuel 15:29, *The Message*). God is with us in these battles, and he gives us wisdom to help us take control of our thoughts. We get to make the choice of which thoughts we will listen and respond to.

"Be strong in the Lord [be empowered through your union with Him]; draw your strength from Him [that strength which His boundless might provides]" (Ephesians 6:10, AMP).

~

When Robert began receiving blood transfusions, I can't begin to express the battle that took place in my mind. The doctor and nurses reassured us that the blood was processed thoroughly and was very safe—we had no reason for concern. But immediately, my mind was flooded with the frightening thought of Robert contracting HIV or Hepatitis. I was tempted to worry that after receiving so many units of red blood cells, he would have complications from an overload of iron. The fearful thought that Robert would have an allergic reaction was also front and center in my mind. I had never even heard of this before the nurse explained to us why she had to wait with him for a period of time at the beginning of each transfusion.

If I had accepted and dwelled on the negative thoughts as Robert received each transfusion, I would have been miserable. I would have worried and become down and depressed. I would have been very unpleasant to be around—and I certainly wouldn't have been any encouragement to Robert.

Thankfully, God speedily came to my rescue by making me aware that to survive the thoughts in my head, I was going to have to take action! I began by praying over each unit of blood as the nurses prepared to administer it to Robert. I would look at the blood or platelets and silently ask God to cleanse it of any impurities and allow Robert's body to accept the transfusion without any complications. There were only a couple of occasions that I was not able to be with Robert when he received his transfusions. But those times I couldn't be present, he would call to keep me informed, and I would still pray over the blood. I prayed over every unit of blood and platelets—all 144 of them.

I also focused on the people who had donated the blood and platelets. Although their names were unknown, I thanked God for each one of them and their families and asked Him to bless them. These people had sacrificed precious time out of their lives to donate, and they were literally keeping the love of my life alive.

The importance of these donors was never more evident than the day, after receiving alarming lab results, Robert had to wait many hours to receive a much needed platelet transfusion. His platelets, which are components of whole blood that help in clotting, had fallen to a dangerously low level. Imagine our concern when we were regretfully informed that there were no platelets available!

Most people are unaware of the great demand for platelets each day. I was certainly not aware and was completely uneducated on the subject. The life span of a platelet is much shorter than any other component of whole blood which makes the demand much greater. We regularly witnessed cancer patients at the transfusion center also receiving platelet transfusions due to chemotherapy.

I was also unaware that apheresis, which is the process of harvesting platelets, is quite time consuming. Donors sacrifice 1 to 2 hours out of their day with each donation.

Although Robert's transfusion was only delayed for the day, that experience was definitely a reminder of our dependence on the selfless sacrifice of others. Our hearts go out to the many people in the world who must wait days or sometimes longer for lifesaving transfusions.

Through the sacrifice of the blood and platelet donors, Robert is alive and it was an honor to pray for those donors and their families. They were—and still are—our heroes!

As I spent time with God at the beginning of those transfusions in prayer, my focus turned to Him. He renewed my mind and gave me peace. As I turned my fears over to God, my mind no longer processed the negative thoughts. At the same time, I was showing Him that I trusted Him with the blood supply and with Robert.

God protected Robert, and he never once had any complications with the transfusions. Six months after Robert's last transfusion, his blood was tested. Of course, the test results were all good, and there were no problems. God is awesome! He also protected me in the battle of my thoughts, and my mind was at peace. God faithfully fought our battles for us.

"The Lord will fight for you, and you shall hold your peace and remain at rest" (Exodus 14:14, AMP).

Do you believe that the thoughts which led to my actions of praying over the blood and donors during Robert's transfusions were my idea? These thoughts were positive and productive, and I believe that they could only have come from God.

> "For though we live in the world, we do not wage war as the world does. The weapons we fight with are not the weapons of the world. On the contrary, they have divine power to demolish strongholds. We demolish arguments and every pretension that sets itself up against the knowledge of God, and we take captive every thought to make it obedient to Christ" (2 Corinthians 10:3–5, NIV).

Born to Fly

I am a strong believer that everything in life happens for a reason. For example, why did you read this book? Do you believe that it was your idea? Is it possible that the idea came from God? Maybe the mere fact that you thought it was your idea is a type of an illusion.

Let me remind you of a verse that I mentioned earlier in Luke 18:19, "'Why do you call Me good? No one is good except God alone'" (NASB).

Keeping in mind that we do nothing good apart from God, could it be that every positive thought which crosses our minds is coming from God? Could it then be possible that every act of kindness, which is produced by positive thoughts, is originated by God?

Could all of those people who say they can't hear from God possibly now consider that they have been hearing from Him all along but just didn't recognize it was Him?

Let's take into account what the Word says in Jeremiah 29:11–13: "'For I know the plans I have for you,' declares the LORD, 'plans to prosper you and not to harm you, plans to give you hope and a future. Then you will call upon me and come and pray to me, and I will listen to you. You will seek me and find me when you seek me with all your heart'" (NIV).

Let's say you acknowledge that God has a good plan for your life. You have chosen to listen to the positive thoughts in your mind as you make choices in your life, acknowledging that you are hearing from and listening to God. Would this mean that you would stay in His will and actually travel down the path that He has planned for you?

On the flip side, if you found yourself in an unfavorable position or bad circumstance, perhaps you could consider that you chose to listen to the wrong voice and are not on the path that God had planned for you. Could you be missing out on blessings that He had for you by making these wrong choices? Please don't misunderstand me; I am certainly not insinuating that every bad or unfavorable circumstance in which we find ourselves throughout our lives is brought on only by our bad choices. But I do believe that *some* of our bad choices directly reflect on our lives and can lead us into bad circumstances.

Is it possible that you are in a bad circumstance in your life right now and are very angry with God? Maybe you have been blaming Him. Could you be directing your anger in the wrong direction? Would you consider that maybe you have made wrong decisions or choices by listening to negative thoughts? Maybe those choices placed you in this position instead of God.

Again, let me remind you that I am not insinuating that every bad or unfavorable circumstance in which we find ourselves is brought on only by our bad choices. For a moment, let's consider Robert and his disease. I don't believe that we did anything to put ourselves on this path. Yet neither do I believe that God brought this disease into our lives.

You might be wondering if we ever question why this has happened to us. Well, the answer for me is *yes*. I questioned and searched for God's motives to why He allowed this disease to take over our lives. I didn't spend very much time dwelling on it, but I did at first question Him. I feel that over time He has revealed to me the answers to my questions with the following thoughts. One morning last year, I woke up from a dream, and I immediately jumped up and wrote this in my journal:

> Baby birds are extremely happy sitting in their nest. It is such a great place to be. The mommy and daddy birds care and provide for the babies, and by the time they are prepared to leave the nest, the babies seem very content staying right where they are. But their parents know

> that it would not be in their best interest to stay in the nest for obvious reasons. If the young birds stayed in the nest, then they wouldn't be able to accomplish what God created them to do. So the parents see to it that those babies get out of the nest and learn to fly.
>
> I think that is kind of what God has done with Robert and me through this disease. We were perfectly happy with our life. It was a very comfortable and wonderful place to be. God had been developing this great relationship with us, and we had been learning so much about Him. We were so blessed and would have been very happy and content staying in that place in our lives forever. But I think that if God had allowed us to stay there, we wouldn't have been able to accomplish what He created us to do. He *allowed* us to be pushed out of our nest, so to speak. We were pushed out of our comfortable, predictable, controlled environment and into an unpredictable, uncertain circumstance with this disease. There we would spread our wings, and He would teach us to fly with Him on our faith and our developed relationship with Him.

"But those who wait for the Lord [who expect, look for, and hope in Him] shall change and renew their strength and power; they shall lift their wings and mount up [close to God] as eagles [mount up to the sun]; they shall run and not be weary, they shall walk and not faint or become tired" (Isaiah 40:31, AMP).

As birds are learning to fly for the first time, their wings are perfectly created and fully developed, with each feather strategically placed. God created them to be prepared to fly as they are sent out or pushed out into the world. He has given them everything they need to eventually soar high in the sky.

God's plan for us is perfect. He strategically allows us to go through experiences which teach us about His character and develop a special relationship with Him. With each experience, a lesson is learned, and our faith grows stronger. Each experience is perfectly timed to develop a spirit which is so in tune with His that the glory of God is revealed through us. As others witness our reactions in bad circumstances and we are filled with the fruit of the Spirit, God and His glory are revealed. This relationship with God, which has been made available to us, is a perfect relationship through Jesus, and is just like those perfectly handcrafted wings.

These wings, which represent a relationship with Jesus, are available to anyone who is willing to accept them. The Word tells us in Romans 10:9–10, "If you declare with your mouth, Jesus is Lord, and believe in your heart that God raised him from the dead, you will be saved. For it is with your heart that you believe and are justified, and it is with your mouth that you confess and are saved" (NIV).

Do you think that the young birds ever question whether the wings they have grown will really support them when they are forced out of the nest? Or do they jump out on faith and count on the fact that they will be lifted and carried high, trusting that they will be safe?

Our relationship with God is solid and will always be what we need—exactly when we need it. The Word promises us in Hebrews 13:5–6 (NIV), "God has said, 'Never will I leave you; never will I forsake you.' So we say with confidence, 'The Lord is my helper; I will not be afraid. What can mortals do to me?'"

> As I think about how God allowed Robert and me to be "pushed out" into an uncertain and challenging life with this disease, I feel that God is teaching us to fly higher using our faith and a developed relationship with Him. We know that this is our opportunity to show Him that we trust Him by looking to Him with childlike faith. We better understand Him as we experience His presence and grace through every difficult situation. Our relationship and love for Him deepens, and our wings of faith grow. He is allowing us to soar high with Him, and He is taking us places we never knew existed! "But he said to me, 'My grace is sufficient for you, for my power is made perfect in weakness.' Therefore I will boast all the more gladly about my weaknesses, so that

> Christ's power may rest on me. That is why, for Christ's sake, I delight in weaknesses, in insults, in hardships, in persecutions, in difficulties. For when I am weak, then I am strong" (2 Corinthians 12:9–10, NIV).
>
> I can now better relate to the meaning of these verses. I don't want to waste this precious gift of life that God has given me by living in fear, doubt, and disbelief. I want to continue to soar higher with life's every challenge. I want to live the great life that Jesus suffered and died on the cross for me to have. So we embrace and celebrate this path that we are walking in our life. Actually, we are not walking, but we are flying very high with God on a level that we have never known before.

After gaining this understanding, I have never again questioned the Lord about aplastic anemia. You see, I do believe that God *allowed* this disease into our lives, because He could teach and grow us while accomplishing His purposes.

Could it be that one of His purposes through this disease was to lead me to write this book? Would you consider that my family is dealing with this disease so that this book would be available for *you* to read at this particular time in *your* life?

Maybe you already believe in God, and you have experienced Him in similar or even mightier ways than my family. Perhaps you are someone who believes in God, but you just don't seem to see Him active in your life. You just can't feel His presence anymore—or maybe you never have. Maybe you are not sure that you even believe in God at all. Has the thought ever crossed your mind that maybe you didn't pick up this book by chance?

Check out this verse in John 15:16 (NIV): "You did not choose me, but I chose you and appointed you so that you might go and bear fruit—fruit that will last."

This verse in John 6:44 also says that Jesus said, "No one can come to me unless the Father who sent me draws them" (NIV).

Could it be possible that God wanted you to spend time with Him? Maybe He wanted your attention. Is it possible that you are living your life believing in and being totally consumed by the enemy's illusions?

You may be thinking that if having God in your life means He allows bad things to happen, then you don't want anything to do with this way of living. If you haven't had this thought yet, you probably will eventually. This thought is negative and is coming from only one place.

The truth is that you will be put into bad circumstances in life—with or without God. The enemy is alive and well, and he wants to destroy you! He most certainly doesn't want you to have a relationship with God and be happy. But the good news is that when you do go through difficulties in your life, God will be there with you. If you seek and trust Him, He will take care of you.

The shocking truth is that we all live in a world filled with the enemy's illusions. I can't help but wonder how much of my life the enemy has influenced and how many blessings I have missed because of his deceit.

Since Robert's diagnosis, I have developed an intimate relationship with God and understand now when He is speaking to me. Robert and I are very happy. We have accepted and love the life that God has given us. I can't begin to express how amazing it feels to know beyond a shadow of a doubt that you are living in God's will and living out your destiny. You won't find anything in this world which will give you that kind of satisfaction at the end of the day other than God.

"Taste and see that the LORD is good; blessed is the one who takes refuge in him" (Psalm 34:8, NIV).

God has a wonderful plan for *your* life, and He loves *you* unconditionally. Keep in mind that I didn't say you will have a problem-free life if you are in a relationship with God. Jesus tells us in John 16:33 (NIV), "In this world you will have trouble. But take heart! I have overcome the world."

Approach every problem with an attitude of faith. Look at each problem as an opportunity to grow spiritually and develop a closer walk with Him. Praise Him, speak and believe His promises through those problems, and you will experience God in a mighty way. As you patiently wait for Him to get you through the problem, you will allow Him the opportunity to love on you. Through this experience, you will better understand the unconditional love He has for you. God's love is huge!

Living in the truth and in a relationship with Christ is amazing. This great way of life is a gift from your Father, and He wants you to have it. Live a life of confidence, knowing that Jesus has overcome the world—and through Him, so can you!

> "I have great confidence in you; I take great pride in you. I am greatly encouraged; in all our troubles my joy knows no bounds" (2 Corinthians 7:4, NIV).

I Shall Not Be Moved

One of my favorite NFL football players is Peyton Manning. He is an amazing quarterback, and I really enjoy watching him play. It is my understanding that when he is not on the field, he is sitting on the sidelines, reviewing plays and continuously striving to learn more about his competitors. He is very successful and at the top of his game.

We have established that succeeding in the battles of our lives requires a conscious effort on our part. We have to stay alert and aware. Becoming well versed in God's character and familiar with the enemy's strategy is essential to our defense.

I don't know about you, but when I hear the word *defense,* I automatically think of sports. Football is actually my favorite sport, and I find watching an occasional football game very enjoyable. I grew up with two wonderful older brothers who taught me how to play the game at a very young age. My brothers placed a helmet on my head before I was big enough to pick up a helmet, much less wear it. They were always kind and very patient with me and included me in their football games with the neighborhood kids in the backyard. They mastered the art of somehow convincing me that I was actually an important part of their team. The huddles were actually some of my most memorable times during our games. We would group together and plan our strategy to defeat our adversaries.

How does a team of football players prepare for their defense? Players spend time learning and planning their strategies as they prepare for their games. They not only spend time with the other members of their team learning strategies and memorizing plays, but also a great deal of time getting to know their opponent. They study the other team to learn and prepare for how they will react and what they will do. When players become more familiar with the other team, they are able to provide their best defense.

In Psalm 62:2, the Word of God tells us that God is our defense. "He only is my Rock and my Salvation, my Defense and my Fortress; I shall not be greatly moved" (AMP). How do we apply this to our lives? How does God act as our defense?

As my husband and I have faced the challenges that accompany aplastic anemia, I have actually used Psalm 62:2 as my defense. I have focused on this promise from God after every setback and have chosen to not allow my feelings and fears to get the best of me. By speaking and believing this verse instead of being consumed by the stress of the setback, I have allowed God to be my defense. My faith in Him protects and defends me. I remain at peace, totally depending on God to fight this battle of aplastic anemia that threatens my precious life with Robert.

I've found that our most important defense is God's Word and believing and standing on His promises. The scripture tells us that the Word of God is the "sword of the Spirit" (Ephesians 6:11–17). The Bible is our arsenal of defense, and it supplies us with everything we could ever need for any situation.

His Word rescued me from the flood of fear that consumed me on the first day as I drove to the hospital to meet Robert at the Cancer Center. I arrived at the doctor's office, and Romans 8:28 rang in my head. The verse calmed me and strengthened me as I felt the Lord's presence.

I have never been one to be able to memorize scripture and retain it. I have tried all my life with no success. I suppose I had just accepted that I wasn't gifted in this area. But during this time, God had led me to place scriptures on my mirror. These verses would be my lifelines in the days to come.

That morning, I had received a phone call from Robert. He was on his way to the oncologist's office at the hospital. He had finally gone to see his doctor secretively, and after going to the lab and receiving a call from the doctor, he was instructed to go straight to the hospital and to be very careful on the way. The doctor had informed Robert that his blood counts were dangerously low and he thought Robert had leukemia.

God's Word was immediately on my mind. I had been getting ready for the day when I received the call, so it took me a few minutes to finish getting dressed. As I completed this task, my hands shook. I began to think to myself, "This is it. This is where the rubber meets the road! Do I believe and trust God or not?"

I immediately started praying, and I felt the grace and presence of God overwhelmingly. Within minutes, the verse that God had apparently led me to place on my mirror spoke to me very strongly.

> "And we know that in all things God works for the good of those who love him, who have been called according to his purpose" (Romans 8:28, NIV).

These words of God came alive and seemed to comfort me. They were like a rope that had been thrown and tied to me to save me from being blown away by the wind of this upcoming storm. They rang in my head very strongly all that day.

As I pulled into the parking lot of the hospital that morning, I remember thinking, "This is so unbelievable. Is this actually happening?" Only a month before, I had visited my doctor for my yearly physical in the building next door. As I parked and walked into the building that day, I couldn't seem to stop looking at the words "Cancer Center" written in large letters on the building beside me. Somehow, I knew deep in my heart that it was only a matter of days before we would be visiting this building.

What took place over the next few days was like an out-of-body experience. I remember speaking to God, saying, "Okay, God, here we go. I know that You will help me deal with whatever is next."

As I entered the doctor's office, I was immediately met by a childhood friend whom I had not seen for many years. It was so comforting to see a familiar face at this moment. She escorted me to the examining room where Robert was waiting. I was very aware of the expressions on the faces of the nurses and employees in the office. I didn't have to wonder what or how they were feeling about the situation.

As I walked down the hall, I remember being very determined that I was going to be strong through God and His grace. I knew that Robert needed to see God's strength in my actions. I knew that I could count on God, because He had held my hand and carried me through my dad's cancer, treatments, and death so gracefully. That journey taught me so much about God. I knew that He was faithful and wouldn't let me down.

I also was painfully aware that Robert was as scared (if not more scared) as I was, but he was leaning on God for his strength also. As I stepped into the examining room, it was very comforting to see God's grace and power in Robert's calm demeanor. I watched Robert and the nurses carry on a conversation as they prepared to do a test on him. I could see God's strength shine gloriously through Robert as he calmly sat and waited.

As they prepared him to do a bone marrow test, I knew that I was barely holding it together and witnessing the doctor stick a very long needle into the love of my life would be more than I could take at that moment. I stepped out into the hallway just outside the door. My kind friend came over to me and said, "Tess, are you okay?" All I really remember saying to her was, "Yes, I'm all right, because I keep hearing this Scripture in my head." I began to quote it to her, word for word, as if I had memorized it. It was very strange and amazing at the same time. For years, I had tried to memorize scripture and failed—yet I had just quoted the verse. I knew that I didn't do this on my own. I knew that it was God and His amazing grace.

From that moment on, I knew without a shadow of a doubt that nothing was going to happen that I couldn't handle with God and His Word. This verse—along with many others—stayed with me and is now a part of me. I desperately clung to these verses for months afterward, and I continue to cling to the Scriptures. I would have much rather had them than food and water. I know this may sound quite dramatic—but it is the truth. These verses are food to my soul, and they have so much power in them. I am living out the Scriptures, and His Word is what I stand on every day as I walk down this path.

Another particularly strong experience with the Word occurred when Robert was preparing to start his chemotherapy treatments. As we prepared for our stay at the hospital, the fear I was experiencing was unbelievable. I was so afraid that he wouldn't survive the treatment. Our doctor had prepped us and shared all the dangers that were involved, and the enemy was working overtime in my mind. Once again, the Word rescued me and gave me the strength and courage that I so desperately needed.

After spending time with God one morning, I was led to this verse:

> "Have not I commanded you? Be strong, vigorous and very courageous. Be not afraid, neither be dismayed, for the Lord your God is with you wherever you go" (Joshua 1:9, AMP).

Words do not do justice in explaining just how important this verse became to me! I wrote it on a piece of paper and taped it to Robert's window at the hospital as soon as we arrived. Every time I started to feel afraid, I prayed it out loud, and it never let me down. It was like God Himself was beside me, speaking the words to me personally, and the verse gave me strength and comforted me like nothing else could. I still have the piece of paper on my refrigerator. I have prayed and spoken that verse many times for many different occasions, and it has always strengthened me.

~

> "I anticipated the dawning of the morning and cried (in childlike prayer); I hoped in your Word" (Psalm 119:147, AMP).

~

The more God has shown me about the enemy and how he attempts to intercept our lives, the more curious I have become in trying to understand just how God wants me to respond. I started praying and studying about my response. As I dug into the subject, the Lord reminded me of Jesus and His experience with Satan in the wilderness.

The Bible says in Matthew 4 that Jesus was led by the Holy Spirit into the wilderness to be tempted by the devil. I had to wonder why Jesus would be purposely directed into the wilderness for temptation—and what God was trying to teach me with this example.

The passage goes on to say that Jesus went without food for forty days and nights. I wondered just how many days the human body can live without food. After some research, I found that the common answer was four to six weeks for a healthy, average person. Jesus was pushing the limit with forty days, and I had to then ask myself why He would go so long without eating. I understand that He was fasting, but this was extreme! Maybe it was to push His physical body to the limit and put Himself in the weakest possible state. Did the Holy Spirit want to set an example of Jesus being at one of His weakest moments physically? Could it be that God knew we could relate to Jesus better in this weakened state?

Jesus was very hungry and physically weakened, and the enemy started messing with His mind and putting thoughts in His head. In my opinion, Satan began to play games with Him just like he does with us today. The enemy especially plays games with our minds when we are really tired, not feeling well, or in a bad circumstance.

The enemy challenged Jesus to turn stones into loaves of bread. Satan knew that Jesus was very hungry and wanted Him to prove that He was God's Son. Jesus replied by *speaking* God's Word: "Man shall not live and be upheld and sustained by bread alone, but by every Word that comes forth from the mouth of God" (Matthew 4:4, AMP).

What was He trying to say? Was it simply a reminder of how important and powerful God's Word actually is? God never intended for us to live the life that He planned for us without His Word. Just as we need food to nourish our physical bodies, we need God's Word to nourish and sustain our spirits.

Notice that Jesus *spoke* God's Word, using it as a defense in the enemy's game. Have you ever really thought about what Jesus did? He used a scripture from Deuteronomy 8:3 to counteract the enemy's temptation. When I think about this, it really amazes me. Jesus actually studied and spoke the same words that are in the Old Testament of my Bible! How great is that? These same words have not changed over thousands of years, and they are the very words that people have sacrificed their lives to preserve. It is so incredible that God's Word has transcended the ages and has never changed or been destroyed! That had to take supernatural power. What a privilege to own a copy of God's sacred Word!

"The grass withers and the flowers fall, but the word of our God endures forever" (Isaiah 40:8 NIV).

Next, the devil tried to get Jesus to jump off the pinnacle of a temple, and he quoted a verse from Psalm 91:11 to persuade Jesus. The enemy actually used God's Word to tempt Jesus. Satan will stop at nothing to try to deceive us (see 2 Corinthians 11:14). In my opinion, this is a great example of why we need God as our umpire in these games—we need His discernment. Jesus then again *spoke* God's words from Matthew 4:7, which are drawn from Deuteronomy 6:16: "It is written also, 'You shall not tempt, test thoroughly, or try exceedingly the Lord your God'" (AMP).

What was Jesus actually saying, and how can we relate this to our lives? Maybe this was a reminder that it isn't such a great idea to mess with the Creator of the universe. Could it possibly mean that you can't expect God to bless your life if you are living in a way that goes against what His Word teaches? When you seriously consider this, if we are living against what God's Word teaches, aren't we basically testing or trying God?

The scripture tells us that the enemy once again tempted Jesus by taking Him up on a very high mountain and showing Him all the kingdoms of the world. The enemy then said he would give them to Jesus if Jesus would worship him. Jesus responded to Satan again by *speaking* God's Word from Matthew 4:10: "For it has been written, you shall worship the Lord your God, and Him alone shall you serve" (AMP). This is drawn from Deuteronomy 6:13: "You shall [reverently fear the Lord your God and serve Him and swear by His name [and presence]" (AMP).

Jesus used God's Word to overcome these temptations from Satan. Notice what Satan said to Jesus about all the kingdoms of the world. He told Jesus that he would give them to Him if Jesus would worship him. Do you believe if Jesus had done what Satan was asking that Satan would have actually kept his word?

This is a great example of an illusion from the enemy. It is very similar to how Satan tempts us today. The enemy is very deceptive. He paints a perfect picture for us of how we can work hard and invest all of our time and energy into things of this world and find happiness. Isn't it an illusion that we can have it all by taking control of our own lives and doing things our own way? Doesn't he often tempt us to believe that although it might mean compromising to get ahead or succeed, we should go for it and strive for worldly recognition?

The enemy tempts us to do things his way—against the Word of God. In Proverbs 16:3, we are told, "Commit to the LORD whatever you do, and your plans will succeed" (NIV). In Psalm 84:11, the Word states, "The Lord God is a Sun and Shield; the Lord bestows [present] grace and favor and [future] glory (honor, splendor, and heavenly bliss)! No good thing will He withhold from those who walk uprightly" (AMP).

In Jeremiah 29:11, we hear, "'I know the plans I have for you,' declares the LORD, 'plans to prosper you and not to harm you, plans to give you hope and a future'" (NIV). I'm sure by now you have noticed that this verse in Jeremiah is very special to my family. You will see this verse mentioned several times throughout this book.

The Word actually tells us that God made a covenant, or promise, with Abraham. I have heard many ministers throughout my life speak of this covenant, but I never really understood it until recently. God has made us promises, but because of our lack of knowledge about the truths of God's Word, we are easy targets for the enemy.

In Genesis 22:17–18, God tells Abraham, "I will surely bless you and make your descendants as numerous as the stars in the sky and as the sand on the seashore. Your descendants will take possession of the cities of their enemies, and through your offspring all nations on earth will be blessed, because you have obeyed me" (NIV).

In Galatians 3:29, the Word says, "And if you belong to Christ [are in Him Who is Abraham's Seed], then you are Abraham's offspring and [spiritual] heirs according to promise" (AMP).

In Acts 3:25, the Word also tells us, "And you are heirs of the prophets and of the covenant God made with your fathers. He said to Abraham, 'Through your offspring all peoples on earth will be blessed.'" (NIV).

Scripture also says, "Because of this oath, Jesus has become the guarantee of a better covenant" (Hebrews 7:22, NIV).

In Jeremiah 32:40, the Word declares, "I will make an everlasting covenant with them: I will never stop doing good to them, and I will inspire them to fear me, so that they will never turn away from me" (NIV).

Keep in mind the fear that this verse is referring to is reverential fear. Jesus deserves our awe and respect. David best describes this in Psalm 34:9–10: "O fear the Lord, you His saints [revere and worship Him]! For there is no want to those who truly revere and worship Him with godly fear. The young lions lack food and suffer hunger, but they who seek (inquire of and require) the Lord [by right of their need and on the authority of His Word], none of them shall lack any beneficial thing" (AMP).

We are also told, "The Angel of the Lord encamps around those who fear Him (who revere and worship Him with awe) and each of them He delivers" (Psalm 34:7, AMP).

These verses make it very clear that God not only wants His children to succeed, but He also wants to bless us. Although, let me bring to your attention a couple of things that we must keep in mind. The world's idea of success is very different from God's.

In God's economy, success isn't measured by the house you live in, the car you drive, or even the degree you've acquired. Success is defined first and foremost by our relationship with Jesus and the fulfillment of the Father's will for our lives.

Please also note that in reality, many of God's blessings are not monetary. He showers His children with a wide variety of spiritual gifts.

The peace and love God provides His children are priceless—and these things are just the beginning of the countless blessings that await those in a relationship with Jesus.

Also notice that in Genesis 22:18 God tells Abraham that He would bless the nations because of his obedience. Obedience is a very important part of receiving blessings from God. He wants us to find success by doing things His way and by letting Him direct our lives.

The Message illustrates this point well: "When John realized that a lot of Pharisees and Sadducees were showing up for a baptismal experience because it was becoming the popular thing to do, he exploded: 'Brood of snakes! What do you think you're doing slithering down here to the river? Do you think a little water on your snakeskins is going to make any difference? It's your life that must change, not your skin! And don't think you can pull rank by claiming Abraham as father. Being a descendant of Abraham is neither here nor there. Descendants of Abraham are a dime a dozen. What counts is your life. Is it green and blossoming? Because if it's deadwood, it goes on the fire'" (Matthew 3:7-10).

God has made promises to us, and it is very important that we are aware and understand that we are heirs of His promises. These verses also make it clear that we cannot use His promises as an excuse to not obey God. In other words, John is asking whether you are obeying God. Are you living your life His way? Isn't John telling us that we can't expect to live against the Word of God and be blessed?

In Joshua 1:8, God says, "Keep this Book of the Law always on your lips; meditate on it day and night, so that you may be careful to do everything written in it. Then you will be prosperous and successful" (NIV).

These verses prove that we can succeed and lead a very blessed life doing things God's way. We just have to make sure we don't compromise and fall into the traps that Satan sets for us to get ahead. We have to ignore the temptation to believe the illusions from the enemy, and we have to be willing to replace those temptations with the godly promises of our covenant.

These additional verses I love from Isaiah 55 talk about God's promises and provision in our lives:

"Come, all you who are thirsty, come to the waters; and you who have no money, come, buy and eat! Come, buy wine and milk without money and without cost. Why spend money on what is not bread, and your labor on what does not satisfy? Listen, listen to me, and eat what is good and you will delight in the richest of fare. Give ear and come to me; listen, that you may live. I will make an everlasting covenant with you, my faithful love promised to David. See, I have made him a witness to the peoples, a ruler and commander of the peoples. Surely you will summon nations you know not, and nations you do not know will come running to you, because of the LORD your God, the Holy One of Israel, for He has endowed you with splendor.

Seek the LORD while He may be found; call on Him while He is near. Let the wicked forsake their ways and the unrighteous their thoughts. Let them turn to the LORD, and He will have mercy on them, and to our God, for He will freely pardon.

'For My thoughts are not your thoughts, neither are your ways My ways,' declares the LORD. 'As the heavens are higher than the earth, so are My ways higher than your ways and My thoughts than your thoughts. As the rain and the snow come down from heaven, and do not return to it without watering the earth and making it bud and flourish, so that it yields seed for the sower and bread for the eater, so is My word that goes out from My mouth: It will not return to Me empty, but will accomplish what I desire and achieve the purpose for which I sent it. You will go out in joy and be led forth in peace; the mountains and hills will burst into song before you, and all the trees of the field will clap their hands'" (Isaiah 55:1-12, NIV).

After exploring these verses and accounts in history, I can gladly accept that God has given us the perfect example of how we should handle the games the enemy plays with us. God's Word has been given to us to execute God's divine will in our lives and help us to obtain a relationship with "the Beginning and the End" (Revelations 21:6). His Word sustains us!

~

> "And He [further] said to me, 'It is done! I am the Alpha and the Omega, the Beginning and the End. To the thirsty I [Myself] will give water without price from the fountain (springs) of the water of Life. He who is victorious shall inherit all these things, and I will be God to him and he shall be My son'" (Revelations 21:6–7, AMP).

~

The Word of God is alive and true, and it has the power to defeat the enemy if we will just give it the chance by putting it into action in our lives.

> "My son, pay attention to what I say; turn your ear to My words. Do not let them out of your sight, keep them within your heart; for they are life to those who find them and health to one's whole body" (Proverbs 4:20–23, NIV).

Lie Down Beside Him

When it became obvious to me that there was something very seriously wrong with Robert, I began to recognize that although we were walking together down this path, there were going to be times that we were not going to be able to share our thoughts with one another. We have always been very close and have shared our feelings and thoughts with each other, and this was going to be new territory for us.

After Robert's diagnosis, I realized how completely different our lives were going to be and that there were going to be times when I would have to deal with things from a totally new perspective. Although we were right beside each other, and God was always present with us, I felt like we were sort of separated—each in our own individual place. There were many times that I felt very alone. I knew God was right there with me, but I had an empty place in my heart that I felt no one really understood. I was very aware that Robert was also in the same situation, as he had to face the complications and treatment of this disease. There was really no way that I could ever understand how he really felt.

For the first time in my marriage, I was in a position where I felt that I could not lean on Robert. The harsh reality that he could possibly die was hard to swallow, and I knew that I had to be strong for him. The fact that I could be left behind was very intimidating. Robert has always been there to support me and lift me up in every situation—which he has continued to do through this whole experience. I just had never actually realized that I had been turning to Robert instead of God for the majority of my support and comfort until this time. But with this situation, even as hard as Robert tried, I had no choice but to turn to God—and God alone—for my comfort and strength. It was during this time that I became familiar with a love and a relationship with the Lord that I never knew existed.

I remember that my greatest comfort during this time was focusing on God and not my circumstances. I realized that I had to put the faith that God had given me into action and just focus on His promise of working everything out for my good—no matter what. It was very comforting for me to realize that I could take Him at His Word and be confident that He would never let me down. I actually came to the realization that it might not be God's will to allow Robert to survive this disease. I had to give in and trust that my Father knew what was best for us. You might call this my moment of truth. I remember it was at this point, that I entered into a level of intimacy with the Lord which I had never known. I entered into a place of rest with God which was like no other. At this point, I knew beyond a shadow of a doubt that His promises were true, and all that I had to do was trust Him to take care of me.

Satan didn't want me to do this, of course. I was tempted with many horrible thoughts of destruction. I had to choose to reject those thoughts and rest in God's promises.

Over the past few years, I have found that another one of my most powerful weapons in my defense is worshipping God through prayer. I feel that God had prepared me in the days prior to Robert's diagnosis with the understanding of how important it is to spend time praising and thanking God—even in uncomfortable circumstances. So I immediately began putting this into action right from the beginning. As I spent time praising and worshiping God, I began to feel His presence in a strong way. I came to the realization that my worship actually brought me into the presence of the Lord. I just had never gotten this revelation before. Every time I became consumed by fear and felt helpless, I would turn my focus from my circumstance to God.

As I reflect back over the last few years and share my God experiences and our life with this disease, I hope you notice that I mention the act of worship many times. Robert and I have spent a lot of time refocusing our attention to God and spending time praising and thanking Him when we were in unfavorable circumstances. I can't explain how, but when we do this, something supernatural happens, and God shows up in a mighty way.

I remember the evening that Robert received a central line catheter in his chest. We were both extremely fearful, but neither of us shared this with the other until months later. When the doctors wheeled him back to the room where they were to do the procedure, a nurse escorted me into a small waiting room. After just a couple of minutes, I was alone in the room.

I believe that God gave me the idea of writing down all the things that I was thankful for while I waited. I wrote the entire time that I was in the room. I had a very long list of the many blessings which God had given me. It was a very intimate time with the Lord—one I will never forget. It was as if God was in the waiting room, sitting in the chair beside me. I felt so content spending time with Him, letting Him know how amazing He was and how thankful I was for everything that He had blessed me with.

Before I knew it, my little beeper went off, notifying me that the procedure was over, and I was able to go back and sit with Robert. The procedure went very smoothly, and he had no complications. I still have the piece of paper that I wrote the praises on that day in my purse. I can't stand the thought of throwing it away.

Another memorable day was one of the days that Robert received his chemotherapy. He was to receive four days of ATGAM, given intravenously. Along with those treatments, he also was to take Cyclosporin and Prednisone. The possible reactions and side affects were very intimidating, and we both trusted God to take care of Robert.

The doctor had informed us that Robert's temperature could rise as high as 105. His fever was at 102 and rising, and I was very concerned. It is extremely hard to watch the love of your life become violently ill and not know whether he will survive. I knew that anything could happen. The anaphylaxis kit which was carefully placed beside his bed didn't help matters.

Robert felt so bad that he couldn't stand any noise in the room. I sat quietly beside him, wondering how I was going to tolerate watching him get sicker by the moment. I had no idea just how ill he would become and how his body would react. I can easily say that this was the most helpless that I have ever felt in my whole life.

The thought suddenly crossed my mind to switch my focus on God, and I sat quietly praying and worshiping Him. I thanked Him for everything I could possibly think of. I thanked Him for the fact that I knew He was in control and He would take care of us—no matter what happened. I begged God to comfort Robert and help him to feel better. I also told God how great and wonderful I thought He was, and then I spent time praying for my close family and friends. As I spent this time praying, I began to experience the Lord's presence, and I suddenly felt a peace come over me.

Within just a short amount of time, Robert started feeling better, and his fever started going down. It was great! This is one of those times with the Lord that I will never forget. God was so sweet to me, and I felt that He was in the room, sitting beside me. Actually, I really felt that I was in His lap, and He was holding me. It was an amazing experience with Him in one of the worst circumstances of my life.

This same day, I had to step out of the room while housekeeping cleaned Robert's room. As I waited, I walked over to a large window at the end of the hall outside his room. As I stood there looking out the window, I noticed that there was something kind of strange behind the parking lot below. I also noticed that the employees were not parking close to this area. Instead, they were parking in an area which was much farther away and required a much longer walk to get into the building. I wondered why they would park so much farther away when those spaces were so much closer.

About one or two minutes later, I turned around and noticed this man walking up the hall. He waved and smiled at me, and I quickly recognized him as he drew closer. It was the young gentleman who had wheeled my husband downstairs when Robert had received his port during our last stay at the hospital. When the man came close enough to speak, he asked me how Robert was doing. He was a very friendly, kindhearted young man who seemed very compassionate and truly concerned with Robert's condition. I gave him an update, and we spoke for a couple minutes. He then turned and looked out the window and asked me if I had been looking at the body farm. I looked at him curiously, and with a smile, I responded by saying, "I don't know what you are talking about." He then described what the area was that I had been so curious about and explained why people wouldn't park in that area.

Apparently, the Anthropological Research Facility from the College of Arts and Science at the University of Tennessee was behind the fence in this area. This facility is also known as the body farm. I had been looking at the entrance of the farm. This facility is used for Forensic Anthropology, which is "the examination of human skeletal remains for the medical-legal community".[1]

The parking places which were near the body farm were not being used because of the odor. Employees would rather park further (and I mean much further) away than smell the farm. I told him that I had just been standing at the window, wondering what the area was and why people wouldn't park around it. After finishing his explanation, he told me that he had to get back to work. We said our goodbyes, and he wished us well as he started walking back down the long hallway.

I was in shock. I knew immediately that God had sent him to me just to answer my questions. It wasn't even important that I knew these things. It didn't even matter. But God had sent him all the way down this long hallway and had interrupted his work so that he could fill me in on the parking lot out back. I knew beyond a shadow of doubt that he was there because God just wanted to reveal to me that He was right there with me, and He was willing and able to do what I needed.

I was so overcome by the presence of the Lord at that moment. After that experience, I was totally relaxed for the rest of the day. I was in awe of the intimacy that God was showing me—and I still can't get over it to this day. God's presence was so beautiful that day, and it still amazes me to think about it! It sounds so crazy to say that God used information about a body farm to reveal Himself to me, but it is true. God is very creative. We can't wrap our minds around how huge and amazing He really is.

"I sought (inquired of) the Lord and required Him [of necessity and on the authority of His Word], and He heard me, and delivered me from all my fears" (Psalm 34:4, AMP).

~

By the way, there is a very important part of the football game which I failed to cover—the job of the umpire. One morning, I heard the following verses read on television by one of my favorite ministers, and it grabbed my attention:

> "And let the peace (soul harmony which comes) from Christ rule (act as umpire continually) in your hearts [deciding and settling with finality all questions that arise in your minds, in that peaceful state] to which as [members of Christ's] one body you were also called [to live]. And be thankful (appreciative), [giving praise to God always]" (Colossians 3:15, AMP).

I decided to do a little research and learn a little more about umpires and their responsibilities. According to *Wikipedia.org,* "The umpire stands behind the defensive line and linebackers observing the blocks by the offensive line and defenders trying to ward off those blocks looking for holding or illegal blocks."[2]

The *American Heritage Dictionary* defines an umpire as "a person empowered to settle a dispute; a judge".[3]

As I mentioned earlier, we need help discerning all of the negative thoughts and questions that arise in our minds. What does it look like to allow the peace from Christ act as our umpire?

Have you ever been totally at peace when suddenly a thought crossed your mind that was stressful and worrisome? Your peace is suddenly gone, and you find yourself thinking about something that is very burdensome. This scripture mentions that God, your umpire, can decide and settle with finality those questions which arise in your mind.

I used to respond negatively to the ridiculous temptations in my head, and I often found myself worrying, which left me stressed out on a regular basis. For most of my life, negative thoughts distracted me, and I innocently dwelled on them. I never even realized that this was taking place. But as I spend more time praying and studying God's Word, He gives me the understanding that I need to become more aware of the temptations. As I receive guidance, I experience a peace from God which I have never known before.

If we allow God to continually stay in our hearts and minds, He will indeed be just like an umpire. Every time a negative thought enters our minds, the Holy Spirit will be there to discern and give us wisdom to reject those thoughts and return to our peaceful state. He will shed light on the deceptive lies of the enemy. Isn't that great? He will do that for us—and all we have to do is be willing to listen to Him. What a relief to know that He is there for us, because we are certainly not capable of understanding all of this on our own.

Notice that the passage goes on to say that we are called to live this way. God wants us to enjoy peace and live in a peaceful state. In Philippians 4:6-7 the Word says, "Do not be anxious about anything, but in every situation, by prayer and petition, with thanksgiving, present your requests to God. And the peace of God, which transcends all understanding, will guard your hearts and your minds in Christ Jesus" (NIV).

What an amazing promise! I am thankful that God has helped me understand and continues to teach me about the deceptive strategies of the enemy. When I choose God's Word and His promises over the ridiculous thoughts in my head, God is faithful! He gives me everything I need to overcome the enemy. With God as our umpire, we can conquer and win this game of life and nothing will keep us from our ordained destiny.

I am amazed at the amount of mercy that God showers on us as we learn and grow with Him. When I think about my life and the way that I was before Robert was diagnosed, I realize that maybe it is possible that Robert's illness was the only way in which God could get my attention and teach me these things.

It is very clear that God's children need to take their spiritual battles more seriously. We need to become familiar with the enemy's strategy, spend more time seeking God, and hide His Word in our hearts so that when we are tempted, we are prepared and do not allow the enemy to keep us from what is best in our lives.

However, we can't do this all alone. We need help understanding and putting this into action in our lives. We need help grasping and holding on to this knowledge. For me, my spiritual eyes sometimes feel like they are blocked or blinded by a thick fog. At times, I can't see or am unaware of what is taking place, but at other times, it is very clear to me what is going on. As I spend more time with God and spend time studying His Word, the fog seems to dissipate, and I see more clearly. As time passes and the fog appears again, it doesn't seem as thick and doesn't reappear as frequently. As my spiritual vision becomes clearer, I then become better able to see the path that God has for me, and I better understand what He wants me to do.

Although the enemy wants you to believe otherwise, God has all of the power! He is our Creator, Father, Redeemer, Savior, Provider, and Healer. I could go on forever about how powerful and amazing God is.

He wants us to come to Him and ask for help. All you have to do is ask Him to help you understand and ask Him to reveal Himself to you. Psalm 34:15, 17 tells us, "The eyes of the LORD are on the righteous and His ears are attentive to their cry; the righteous cry out, and the LORD hears them; He delivers them from all their troubles" (NIV).

This next passage promises us that He will share His knowledge with us. These verses have become very important to me and my family. After we have prayed these verses out loud, He has given us wisdom. We have seen God move in amazing ways. He never fails us, and he always reveals Himself to us just when we need it.

> "For the LORD gives wisdom, and from His mouth come knowledge and understanding. He holds success in store for the upright, He is a shield to those whose walk is blameless, for He guards the course of the just and protects the way of his faithful ones. Then you will understand what is right and just and fair—every good path. For wisdom will enter your heart, and knowledge will be pleasant to your soul. Discretion will protect you, and understanding will guard you" (Proverbs 2:6–11, NIV).

As I am reminded of how we have seen God move through this passage, I can't help but think of the times that I just don't ask Him for help. Have you ever wondered why we don't ask for His help? Is it our pride that keeps us from asking? Maybe it is our lack of faith. Do we believe that God really is who He says He is and that He will do what He says He will do? Or maybe we fear that what we are doing is just not big or serious enough to bother God.

In James 4:2, we are told, "You do not have because you do not ask God" (NIV). We are also told in James 1:6, "But when you ask, you must believe and not doubt, because the one who doubts is like a wave of the sea, blown and tossed by the wind" (NIV).

God loves us so much that He allows us the choice of whether to have Him in our lives. He allows us the freedom to choose. We have to decide who we will believe and who we will put our faith in. The Word even tells us that we have a choice to make. Do we choose to serve the Lord by listening and responding to the voice of God, or do we choose to serve the enemy?

"But if serving the LORD seems undesirable to you, then choose for yourselves this day whom you will serve, whether the gods your forefathers served beyond the River, or the gods of the Amorites, in whose land you are living. But as for me and my household, we will serve the LORD" (Joshua 24:15, NIV).

A while back, a story from the Bible was brought to my attention by a sermon that I watched on television. I had heard this story many times, but on this day, I feel that God opened my eyes and helped it make more sense to me. This account is in Mark 4. It is the story of Jesus asleep in the boat when the disciples were with Him. The storm came, blowing them back and forth. The winds were hurricane-sized, and the water was very dangerous. In other words, it was a very big storm, and the disciples were very afraid!

The disciples woke Jesus up and asked Him why He seemed to not care about the fact that they were in this terrible storm. Jesus didn't understand why they had so little faith and were afraid of the storm with Him right there with them. Jesus ordered the wind to stop, and it did. Jesus ordered the water to calm down, and it did. Wow—how big is that?

On this day, Jesus taught me that He doesn't want us to be afraid when the storms come. The circumstances of our storm might look huge and frightening, but God is bigger than any storm.

Jesus wants us to just have faith, instead of being fearful and freaking out. He wants us to have the kind of faith that looks at the circumstances and chooses to lie down beside Him and rest, be peaceful, and sleep.

Oh, by the way—the boat filled up with water. The disciples were standing in water in the boat! I think Jesus wanted them to just go lie down in the water beside Him and trust that He would take care of them.

This is how I want to live my life! I want to ignore the circumstances and know that God is bigger than any storm. I want to please my God by lying down beside Him—even as the water rises around me in the boat—and resting in my faith in Him!

This was an awesome picture which God gave me that day. This storm of aplastic anemia brings many threatening circumstances into our lives, and it brings potentially threatening circumstances for our future. This disease has the potential to rob me and my family of so much. In the midst of these threatening circumstances, Jesus wants me to understand that He is much bigger than these circumstances. He wants us to rest in this disease—rest beside Him, knowing that He knows what is best for us, He loves us, and He will take care of us. You can't get that kind of peace and security from anything on this earth. It only comes from Jesus, and He is *mighty!*

> "The LORD is righteous in all His ways and loving toward all He has made. The LORD is near to all who call on Him, to all who call on Him in truth. He fulfills the desires of those who fear Him; He hears their cry and saves them" (Psalm 145:17–19, NIV).

Don't Lose Your Flavor

I mentioned earlier that as I spent time with God studying His Word, I began to see things much more clearly in my spiritual life. As things have become clearer, I have been able to hear from God and have a better understanding of what path He has for me. This is an amazing gift.

I feel that God has been teaching me that when I can clearly see what He wants me to do in a situation, there can and will be challenges to stop me. The challenge can actually be obedience. What do I mean by this? Well, when our obedience is required, it almost always carries with it consequences. I have found that as I choose the good path of obedience, the consequences of my obedience are sometimes good and sometimes bad.

The world's ways are very different than God's ways. When I am clearly shown the path that I am to take in a situation and I actually walk down that path, the world doesn't seem to understand. People's feelings and emotions get involved, and others can sometimes react negatively to your actions—even when your acts of obedience are clearly the right thing for you. Sometimes those right choices can actually make *your* emotions feel wrong, even to yourself. But the good news is that if you do the right thing, then God will watch your back and protect you.

"For the LORD will go before you, the God of Israel will be your rear guard" (Isaiah 52:12, NIV).

One late winter evening, I was trying to process and put in perspective the hectic day I had experienced. I was sitting in our family room in front of a warm fire, talking to God. My husband had already fallen asleep, and my daughter was in another room, studying. I had been obedient that day and done something that I knew was what God wanted. Although I had done what I knew was right, I had been unexpectedly treated very badly by someone I loved.

I spent time asking God questions and wondering if I had made some wrong choices or maybe handled the situation differently than He had planned. I begged Him for guidance and then sat silently, waiting for answers.

After several minutes of silence, I decided to turn on the television. As I surfed through the channels, I searched for one of my favorite ministers, who was sometimes broadcast on that day of the week. I told God that I needed understanding, and if I could just hear this minister speak some encouragement, it would help me regain my peace. As I flipped through the channels, I had no success finding the minister. I did, however, stop on a station with another minister speaking, and he was at the end of his sermon. He explained that when you are obedient to God, there will be consequences. He went on to say that you must still be obedient, leave the consequences with God, and trust Him.

I was once again blown away by God and His loving ways. He never ceases to amaze me with His perfect timing, and He never lets me down. Those words were exactly what I needed to hear to answer my questions, and I learned a good lesson that night. I had done what God wanted me to do that day, and I had been shocked by the consequences. God taught me that when He asks me to do something, I simply need to be obedient and leave the consequences with Him. I regained my peace and thanked God for His grace, mercy, and help in understanding.

Why is it that we don't expect there to be consequences for our obedience? When your obedience requires putting God's plan or assignment before the people you care about, there will be consequences—especially from those who are closest to you (see Matthew 10:34–36). Sometimes they will not understand, and they will get angry with you. The enemy will use them to distract you—even though they are saved and have a relationship with God. If they choose to allow their feelings to control their actions and tongues, then their anger will be used as an attack from the enemy.

The good news is you don't have to allow their actions to affect you. If you are aware that there are consequences to your obedience, you will be more alert to the fact that the enemy uses other people's weaknesses to attack you. As you become more aware, you will recognize when this is taking place. You will be tempted to take this attack personally, and your fleshly feelings and emotions will certainly want to give in to the temptation. But with this knowledge, you can choose *not* to take it personally. In turn, you can stop allowing this process to become successful and steal your peace.

We all have a sinful nature. God shows us patience and mercy—yet why is it that we seem to have so little patience and mercy for others? God understands that we are learning and growing and we are all at different levels in our relationships with Him. We receive God's amazing grace, but somehow we just can't seem to share this gift with others—not even our closest family and friends. We expect others to be where we are in our walk with God. We judge others when they do not act like we think they should act or when they act ugly. I am thankful for Jesus, who died on the cross to save us from not only our sins, but from ourselves (see Romans 3:22–26 and 1 John 1:5–8).

I find it interesting that I have such patience and mercy for my own child, but I find it much harder to be that generous with other people. I am amazed at the mercy the Lord has shown me. I have done many things I shouldn't have, knowing that they were wrong. But God always forgives me and loves me unconditionally. Why is it so hard to share this forgiveness and unconditional love with others?

I am constantly tempted to judge and have no mercy for others. My goal is to choose to ignore the temptations and be obedient by doing what God wants me to do—even when I don't feel like it.

As I have grown closer to God, my obedience has caused me to lose some relationships. But God is teaching me that it is to be expected, and it is not my business or responsibility to judge how others respond to my obedience. I have to remember to leave this to God. My responsibility is to pay attention and control how *I* respond to their actions. I cannot control the actions of others, but I *can* control myself with God's help.

This can be extremely challenging, because it is easy to get caught up in the actions of others. The words and actions of other people can sometimes be very hurtful and unexpected. We can then easily become consumed with our emotions and focus on others' reactions instead of our own.

I used to believe that it was my responsibility to react to the bad actions of others—and in turn, to treat them badly as a consequence of their bad treatment. The Lord has taught me through the years that it just isn't my responsibility to judge others and set them straight. However, it is my responsibility to treat people kindly, forgiving them and showing them love and respect—even when they treat me badly.

We have to make a choice to allow God's love and mercy to overcome our feelings. This is very hard to do, but when we succeed in not giving in to our emotions and feelings and do what is right, God is honored! God will, in turn, honor and bless us for our obedience. In Matthew 5:13, the Word says, "You are the salt of the earth; but if the salt loses its flavor, how shall it be seasoned?" (NKJV)

God has shown me that His love is another very important weapon against the enemy. Whether you are in a disagreement with someone or just find yourself in a difficult position or circumstance, allowing God's love to flow through you to others will definitely put the enemy in his place. It is at these times—when we do *not* allow our emotions and feelings to determine how we respond to our circumstances—that the world actually sees God through us.

"Dear friends, let us love one another, for love comes from God. Everyone who loves has been born of God and knows God. Whoever does not love does not know God, because God is love. Dear friends, since God so loved us, we also ought to love one another. No one has ever seen God; but if we love one another, God lives in us and His love is made complete in us" (1 John 4:7–8, 11–12, NIV).

As believers, we represent the Living God. If the world cannot see the love of God and His light through us and our actions, where will they see it? I like to think of believers as lighthouses. God uses us in many different ways to reach out to others. If we are obedient and do things the way He commands, then His light will shine through us.

Those who struggle in the darkness will see the light and want what we have in Jesus.

"Whoever loves his brother [believer] abides (lives) in the Light, and in It or in him there is no occasion for stumbling or cause for error or sin. But he who hates (detests, despises) his brother [in Christ] is in darkness and walking (living) in the dark; he is straying and does not perceive or know where he is going, because the darkness has blinded his eyes" (1 John 2:10–11, AMP).

Always keep in mind that the darkness doesn't like the light. The enemy doesn't want people who are living in the darkness to see the light and turn to it. So he uses anything and everything to stop us from doing the right thing and being obedient. If he can't stop us from being obedient, then he will actually try to counteract our obedience. He can use the people closest to us—if they are not aware of what is going on— to tempt us to be offended and angry. If we aren't aware then we can become angry and retaliate. The enemy's plan of counteracting the light has then succeeded.

If we simply focus on our own actions, being obedient and loving and forgiving others unconditionally, God will take care of the rest. I don't know how you feel, but it is a relief to know that I don't have to be responsible for the actions of others—God doesn't even want to hear my opinion on it. It truly is freeing to not have this responsibility.

Unfortunately, I forget this, and I often tell Him and others how I feel about it. God has shown me that my pride makes me think that I have a right to give my opinion—and my opinion holds weight. I am constantly reminded that my mouth is running—and as Thumper said in the Walt Disney classic *Bambi,* "If you can't say something nice, then you shouldn't say nothin' at all".

I want to always be willing—with the Holy Spirit's guidance—to search every circumstance or bad situation and seek the lessons God has for me. Once again, I am reminded that we all have a choice to make in every situation. Do we listen to the positive and do what God commands, or do we open the door for the devil and dwell on the negative? We all must strive to seek the positive by the help of the Holy Spirit and the wisdom which God gives us.

With God's help, we will be powerful lighthouses, shining His light throughout our families and communities. We will begin to see God do amazing things through us, and I truly believe that this is when we will see Him bless our lives in abundance. I know that since I have allowed Him to control more of my days and been more obedient, He has poured many more blessings on my family.

Keep in mind that it is not possible to do any of this without God's help. The Holy Spirit is with us to empower us. He is with us to help us make the right choices and do the right thing—even when it doesn't feel good or when we know there will be consequences that come along with our obedience. We can't allow those bad feelings or actions of others to stop us from doing what is right.

If we continue to spend time with God, His truth and light will shine through us, and this light will get the attention of others. Many will be led out of the darkness into the amazing light—and into the most awesome relationship with the King of this universe.

"Let your light so shine before men that they may see your moral excellence and your praiseworthy, noble, and good deeds and recognize and honor and praise and glorify your Father Who is in heaven" (Matthew 5:16, AMP).

That night by the fire, after I had spent time thanking God, I snuggled up on the couch with my husband and fell asleep. Before going to sleep, I turned the television to something random to help me settle down and relax. About an hour later, I woke up and realized that it was late and my husband and I needed to go to bed. Guess who was on the television? It was the minister who I had been trying to find earlier. How sweet is our God? It was very late, but I watched the minister and knew that God had given me this gift. To say the least, I slept like a baby that night.

~

> "You are the light of the world. A city that is set on a hill cannot be hidden. Nor do they light a lamp and put it under a basket, but on a lampstand, and it gives light to all who are in the house" (Matthew 5:14–15, NKJV).

~

Many times our acts of obedience not only bless others, but also unexpectedly bless us. I have found these times to be some of my most memorable times with the Lord.

I have discovered that some of my favorite experiences are when the response to my obedience is good and I get to enjoy the blessing that comes along with my obedience. When I find myself in an uncomfortable situation or bad circumstance, the Lord has taught me to invest in, bless, and love others.

When Robert and I were planning for our long stay at the hospital for his treatments and recovery, we felt that if we cooperated with God, He could use us in a very special way. Keep in mind that we believed we had been placed in this circumstance for a reason. As I mentioned previously, I am a strong believer that everything happens for a reason. Therefore, I knew that God must have plans to use us to help others and touch people's lives in a positive way during our stay at the hospital.

We believed (and still do) that when life seems to be suddenly shaken, if you focus on God instead of the problem, He will always give you opportunities to be productive for Him in any situation. As I spent time with the Lord one morning, I felt led to purchase books to give away during our stay at the hospital. One particular book was very special to us—*Fresh Wind Fresh Fire* by Jim Cymbala—so we purchased boxes of these books to take with us to the hospital.

We kept the books hidden under the bed in our hospital room, and we gave them to all of the nurses who cared for Robert during his treatment and recovery. Keep in mind that when we ordered the books, our minds were focused on blessing the nurses, and we had no idea that in return, God would use them to bless us.

Our hearts were filled with anticipation as each new nurse entered our room. The nurses work twelve-hour shifts for several days in a row, so we would have the same nurse for many days. It was an inspiration to witness each nurse be amazed that we were giving him or her a gift. As several of them received their books, their eyes filled with tears as they thanked us. Robert would then share with them how much the book meant to us, that it had changed his prayer life, and the reason we wanted them to have it.

Giving the books away turned out to be a huge, unexpected blessing for us. It seemed to help us deal with the bad experience and gave us something to look forward to every day. It was just one of the many ways God helped us deal with our long stay in the hospital. God's creative ways are a mystery to me.

> "Can you fathom the mysteries of God? Can you probe the limits of the Almighty?" (Job 11:7, NIV)

He Goes Before You

As I watched Robert work to diligently repair our front porch, I stood at the front door with tears streaming down my face, knowing that the man I was watching was extremely ill. I was absolutely terrified, but I didn't say a word to him, because I was determined to allow him the courtesy of dealing with this situation in his own way. I knew that his condition had to be very serious, and I knew that he was struggling to finish the project.

For months before Robert was diagnosed, I had felt God was preparing me for something. It is hard to explain, but I somehow knew we were going to face a great challenge. I felt that we were going to face a health issue and it was going to be very serious. I even remember praying for the unknown path and asking God to prepare us for it and strengthen us.

For some reason, I just assumed it was going to be me with the upcoming health issue. I never dreamed that it would be Robert until he started looking pale and his health began to obviously deteriorate. It sounds very strange, and although I didn't completely understand what was ahead, in my heart, I truly felt God preparing me, and I knew it was coming.

"It is the Lord Who goes before you; He will [march] with you; He will not fail you or let you go or forsake you; [let there be no cowardice or flinching, but] fear not, neither become broken [in spirit–depressed, dismayed, and unnerved with alarm]" (Deuteronomy 31:8, AMP).

~

> "If you are facing challenges that seem overwhelming, don't be discouraged. God has already foreseen them and prepared for them" (Henry R. and Richard Blackaby, *Experiencing God Day-By-Day Devotional).*[1]

~

God has proven to me time and time again that He is always prepared and that He does go before us. In Matthew 6:8, the Word tells us, "Your Father knows what you need before you ask Him" (AMP). God's mysteries never cease to amaze me. They leave me questioning Him and living in a continual state of awe.

I spent a lot of time on the cancer floor at the University of Tennessee Medical Center with my dad when he was treated for cancer. I took him to most of his doctor's appointments and chemotherapy treatments. At the end of his life, when he stayed a couple of weeks in the hospital, I spent a lot of time with him.

During that time, I became very aware of the nursing staff on the cancer floor. It was incredible to me how dedicated and hard-working the nurses were with all of their patients. These nurses have an extremely difficult and challenging job, both physically and emotionally. I could never express in words what the staff meant to me as we slowly watched my dad take up his wings and fly off to heaven.

As I left the hospital the night after my dad's death, I couldn't get the nurses off my mind. I began to pray for them every day. It wasn't something I had to remind myself to do, but instead seemed to be something I had to do. I felt a very strong connection somehow, and I didn't even know a single one of them personally. My obsession with praying for them went on for years.

Years after my dad's death, I was in a prayer group at my church on a Wednesday night. This was in the early years of our church, and we had just moved into our new building. A lady in our group whom I hardly knew began to pray. She mentioned the women on her floor who were struggling and continued to pray for the patients who concerned her. As she prayed, I became aware that she was obviously praying for nurses and cancer patients. I soon became overwhelmed by the fact that she was a nurse on the cancer floor at University of Tennessee Medical Center.

It was amazing that after all the years of praying for these nurses, one would actually show up in this prayer group. I was so touched by her presence that tears began to stream down my face as I tried to compose myself. After the prayer meeting, I asked her a few questions, and she shared a few details of her job. She was actually the manager of the nurses on the cancer floor. I apologized to her for being so emotional and then explained that I had been praying for her and the others for years.

Strangely enough, when I look back at this day, I am amazed at the grace of God. Little did I know that years later, she would be one of my heroes when Robert became ill and received his treatments at UT. God's grace was preparing us as we developed a dear friendship with her and her husband. We consider them some of our most special friends. They ministered to us, and I will always be grateful for all the special attention that was given to us

When Robert was diagnosed with aplastic anemia and we were informed that he was going to receive chemotherapy, I immediately knew that we needed to be with our friend at UT. She would be comforting to me, and I knew that she would provide the very best care for Robert. I am so glad that God reminded me He was preparing the way for us—even then.

As I reflect back and think about God's provision, I am reminded of another special story with one particular nurse on the cancer floor.

The last week of my dad's life, I was convinced that God had sent me an angel. She was a very happy, energetic, spirit-filled nurse who spent some of the last few days with my dad and me. She helped me understand that the end of my dad's life was at hand, and she helped me prepare to let him go. She had a special way about her that was blunt, yet she spoke the truth in such a kind way. She was exactly who I needed to help me deal with the inevitable. She would make comments that would give me exactly what I needed even before I knew that I needed it. I honestly knew that she was a gift from God to help me give up my dad. I really thought she was an angel.

Well, eight years later, guess who walked through the door of Robert's room when we entered the hospital to receive his chemotherapy treatments? That's right—it was my angel!

This reminds me of a funny story. Prior to Robert's illness, I was shopping one day, and I recognized a lady who looked like the angelic nurse. At the time, I didn't know her name. She was at the checkout, and I eagerly ran up to her and started talking to her. She reacted very strangely as I introduced myself and began to explain why I was speaking to her. She in turn responded to me by explaining that I had mistaken her for her sister. You can imagine my surprise and embarrassment when I found out that my angel had a twin sister. I then explained that her sister had helped me with my dad when he was sick with cancer.

Well, when this special nurse walked into Robert's room at the hospital eight years later, I was in shock. My first reaction was to be excited. I began to share the story with her of how I really had been convinced she was an angel God had sent to me during the time of my dad's death. She just laughed, told me a few stories about her life, and told me how much she appreciated my comments.

Within minutes of speaking to her, I became overwhelmed by fear! "Had God sent her to me again for something really bad? Was Robert going to die? Was that why she was there?" It was all too much for me. This couldn't be happening again! Immediately, I started asking God what was happening. I knew that this was no coincidence and God had brought us back together for a reason.

God immediately comforted me with a verse that ran through my mind. It was Psalm 118:17: "I shall not die but live, and shall declare the works and recount the illustrious acts of the Lord" (AMP). I knew by this verse ringing in my head that God had a plan, and I just needed to trust Him and not think ahead.

It wasn't long before I realized she was there to comfort me—and that she did. She is one of the best chemotherapy nurses on the floor. Her years of experience gave me peace, and her wonderful personality was a gift. We got to know her and enjoy her bubbly personality.

I can't tell you how much reassurance and stability her presence gave me those long four days of Robert's treatments. Just knowing that she was there was important to me. I knew that if something went wrong, she would know just what to do. But most of all, I knew that this was no coincidence and God had sent her there for us.

Again, God had sent this dear nurse to assist me in the worst experience I had ever dealt with in my life. The experience of Robert's illness was uncharted territory for me, just as it was eight years ago when I brought my dad into the hospital to die. This may sound dramatic, but I knew my dad would never walk out of the hospital again. I remember pulling the car out of his driveway with him, knowing that it would be the last time he would ever be at his home. I knew that I was taking him to the hospital to die, and I didn't know how I was going to handle it. The only thing I did feel confident about was the fact that I knew God was there with me. I knew that I could trust Him to get me through and show me what to do next. It was one of the hardest experiences of my life until Robert became ill. What I had gone through with my dad suddenly seemed like a cakewalk in comparison.

"And therefore the Lord [earnestly] waits [expecting, looking, and longing] to be gracious to you; and therefore He lifts Himself up, that He may have mercy on you and show loving-kindness to you" (Isaiah 30:18, AMP).

How amazing is our God! He loves us so much that He had already arranged for the special nurse to work that room on those particular days. Why is it that we worry or stress about our lives? God has everything in control, and He stops at nothing to take care of us and bless us in the most intimate ways. He goes before us and makes our paths straight.

> "Trust in the LORD with all your heart and lean not on your own understanding; in all your ways acknowledge Him, and He will make your paths straight" (Proverbs 3:5–6, NIV).

Walking by Faith

After Robert's treatments, the process of waiting for his bone marrow to recover and his blood counts to rise has been a challenging experience. Nothing can prepare you for the reality of just how slow the process really is. The buildup of anticipation that transpires between each visit is very exasperating. This disease is very unpredictable, and without our faith in God, I truly do not know how we would have dealt with it.

From the very beginning of this process, Romans 4:19–21 has fed me with patience and hope. Even after all of these months, it continues to help me deal with the roller coaster of blood counts with aplastic anemia. I love and am so thankful for God's Word. It sustains me and defends me from the enemy that relentlessly lies to me.

> "He did not weaken in faith when he considered the [utter] impotence of his own body, which was as good as dead because he was about a hundred years old, or [when he considered] the barrenness of Sarah's [deadened] womb. No unbelief or distrust made him waver (doubtingly question) concerning the promise of God, but he grew strong and was empowered by faith as he gave praise and glory to God. Fully satisfied and assured that God was able and mighty to keep His word and to do what He had promised" (Romans 4:19–21, AMP).

After Robert's diagnosis, we became painfully aware that his blood counts controlled our days. We were reminded with each doctor's visit that our lives were out of our control. In the beginning, with each visit, our day was planned according to how good or bad his counts were. We spent many days in the transfusion room receiving blood and platelets. Although we were very thankful for the transfusions that were keeping him alive—not to mention thankful for the blood donors who supplied the blood—it was quite an adjustment. But as we adjusted to the inability to plan our days and surrendered to the lack of control, we were reminded and reassured that God was in control of the blood counts on several occasions.

We had a vacation to Destin planned the summer we received Robert's diagnosis, and we weren't able to make the trip. The doctor didn't feel comfortable allowing Robert to go that far away. He just wasn't stable enough for such a long trip away from home. To our surprise, God made sure that we got the opportunity to go on a vacation to Destin the next summer, and it was a much nicer trip than the original trip could ever have been. Some special friends allowed us to spend a week in their very nice condo—free of charge. This condo was so comfortable and was right across the street from the beach.

As we prepared for the trip the week we were supposed to leave, I became apprehensive about going. I was very uncomfortable going that far from Robert's doctor. I began praying that God would give me a sign or somehow let me know that we were definitely meant to go on the trip.

We had our regular checkup on the day before we were to leave for Florida. When we received the results from Robert's lab work, his white cell count had jumped up into the normal range for the first time since his diagnosis. It was my sign, and I was amazed! Not only did we get much-needed time away from our responsibilities, but we got a vacation from aplastic anemia. Since Robert's white cell count was normal, we were able to go out and eat in restaurants, and enjoy shopping and mingling with people in public places with ease. It was a wonderful gift from God. The vacation was very special and we will always be grateful for our friends' generosity.

Isaiah 30:18 says, "Blessed (happy, fortunate, to be envied) are all those who [earnestly] wait for Him, who expect and look and long for Him [for His victory, His favor, His love, His peace, His joy, and His matchless, unbroken companionship]!" (AMP)

On another occasion our daughter was at home sick with a virus which was very similar in symptoms to the flu. She had a very high fever for many days. I began praying immediately when she started feeling under the weather that God would protect Robert. That week, we just happened to have an appointment with Robert's doctor for a regular checkup, and his white cell count was in the normal range.

The month after each of these incidents, his white cell counts fell back down below normal. We are convinced and completely reassured that God is in control of the blood counts. "Wait and hope for and expect the Lord; be brave and of good courage and let your heart be stout and enduring. Yes, wait for and hope for and expect the Lord" (Psalm 27:14, AMP).

As we expectantly wait for the results of Robert's lab work at each doctor's appointment, we always anticipate an improvement. We are that certain of God being who He says that He is and doing what He says He will do! Time and time again, we are given results that do not meet our expectations. But after dealing with a few brief moments of disappointment, we focus on the positive in the situation and rejoice in the fact that Robert is stable and doing well. We no longer have to spend relentless hours getting transfusions or treatments—this is only a dream to most of the patients in the waiting room sitting next to us. We feel confident that God just isn't ready to allow those counts to come up yet. He is in complete control, and we will continue to trust Him. Just as Abraham continued to believe that God would do as He had promised, we believe that the same God will do as He has promised us.

After one particular visit to the doctor about a year and nine months into this disease, Robert and I were once again disappointed by the lab work. His counts had been slowly rising, and at the previous visit, his platelet count had jumped up 25 percent. This was the biggest jump we had ever experienced. His platelet count was on the verge of entering the normal range. On this particular visit, we had anticipated that his platelets would be up in the normal range, but we were informed that they had dropped back down 25 percent.

We never stop getting our hopes up. God gives us the grace and has taught us to not be discouraged. We stand on His Word and are confident that He knows what is best.

We are prisoners of hope and are very confident in this promise from Zechariah 9:12, "Return to the stronghold, You prisoners of hope. Even today I declare that I will restore double to you" (NKJV).

The Lord continues to encourage us as He did that day with a story from the book I had been reading by Joel Osteen, *Your Best Life Now*. In the book, Osteen tells a story about two former college basketball players who were going to Kenya to do mission work. Both of the men were very tall and about twenty-seven years old. They were confident that it was God's will for them to go, and they had people praying for them to have a problem-free trip.

During their flight, there was some bad weather. They missed one of their connecting flights and had to wait eight or nine hours for another flight. When the time came to get on the plane, the only seats available were in first class, so the airline placed them in those seats—right up in the front of the plane. They were pretty happy about that, since they had such long legs. But in the middle of the flight, the plane started going down, and everyone on the plane started freaking out. The young men started praying. As you can imagine, they were really confused about the turn of events. They just didn't understand why—after all the prayer—they were experiencing such terrible circumstances. They then heard some disturbance in the front of the plane, so they went to the door of the cockpit. As the attendant opened the door, they saw a very tall, large man who was attacking the pilots. The young men detained the disturbed man just in time for the pilots to regain control of the plane, saving everyone—including some who would have been killed on the ground from the crash.

Osteen writes, "Sometimes God will put you in an uncomfortable situation so you can help somebody else. God delayed those two young men on purpose. He put them in first class, right up front, so they could help save that entire plane. God knows what He's doing. He can see the big picture; He can see the future. And He has you exactly where

He wants you today. Quit questioning Him, and start trusting Him. Just know that God is in control. He has your best interests at heart. He's directing your steps."[1] "The steps of a [good] man are directed and established by the Lord when He delights in his way" (Psalm 37:23, AMP).

Joel Osteen's book has been a blessing from God. He has used it to encourage me on several occasions. I still need to hear and be reminded on a regular basis that God is in control and that He knows what is best for us.

Proverbs 16:9 reminds us, "In his heart a man plans his course, but the LORD determines his steps" (NIV).

If God had not directed us down the path of this life-threatening disease, we would not have been in the position to experience Him in the amazing ways that we have. We would have missed out on so many awesome experiences with God. We recognize this disease is our opportunity to see God at work and walk by faith. God is the planner of our days, and we know that our paths are designed by the Master of the universe. How could we possible be unhappy with that?

"Trust in the LORD with all your heart and lean not on your own understanding; in all your ways acknowledge him, and he will make your paths straight" (Proverbs 3:5–6, NIV).

~

After Robert's diagnosis, as you can imagine, my family was challenged by some very difficult battles of the mind. During this transition, I felt that everything which I relied on was at risk of being taken from me. It was as if someone jerked a rug out from under my feet.

As I mentioned before, I had to face the fact that Robert might not make it. Everything was at stake—including my life with the man I was madly in love with for over twenty-years, my financial stability, my home, and life as I knew it. Even the insurance company we had Robert's life insurance policies with was at risk of going under. Although I was completely aware that if one life insurance company goes under, others (by law) have to take on the failed company's policies, every time I turned on the television and listened to the news, the stations spoke about the possibility of this company going under. The television reporters were very concerned that if this company failed, it would devastate the economy. The life insurance policies were something that I possibly would not be able to count on due to this company's instability. Everything in my life was up in the air, and I felt very helpless.

I did not realize that I had been leaning on worldly things instead of God for my stability until there was a threat of losing them. I had to make a change and start putting my complete faith in God and God alone. I had to believe that He would provide for all of my needs and would be my rock, provider, and stability!

I recently read a devotional that used the example of a vine on a trellis. This image perfectly expresses how I felt at this time in my life:

> "Oh, how everything gives way when affliction first comes upon us! The clinging stems of our hopes are quickly snapped, and our heart lies overwhelmed and prostrate, like a vine the windstorm has torn from its trellis. But once the initial shock is over and we are able to look up and say, "It is the Lord" (John 21:7), faith begins to lift our shattered hopes once more and securely binds them to the feet of God. And the final result is confidence, safety, and peace" (L. B. Cowman, *Streams in the Desert).*[2]

On one particular day during Robert's recovery, I was driving to the hospital alone in my car. As I began to talk over my fears with God I believe He opened my eyes to several realities.

I came to the painful realization that Robert was not mine—he didn't belong to me. I became very aware that God had total control of His life and mine for that matter. I have always had a special respect for my daughter, and I was very aware that she belonged to God. It had just never really occurred to me that Robert also belonged to God. It was time to come to terms with this reality. I had to accept that God had complete control of whether Robert lived or died.

I also became very aware of the fact that my life had always been in God's hands and my provision had always come from Him and Him alone. All of these years I had experienced a false sense of security with the world. I had been living an illusion of self-sufficiency. I then began to understand that nothing in my life had really even changed except the fact that I was now aware and I had been given a new perspective. What a wonderful gift.

I feel the Lord also revealed to me that most everyone around me was living in this same illusion, but just weren't aware of it. Most everyone lives in this false sense of security. I was reminded that no one is promised tomorrow, and no one knows what even today will bring.

It became very clear to me that I had always been vulnerable to the world and all of the dangers in it, but God had always covered and protected me and my family. I needed to become comfortable depending only on God to supply my *every* need. It was obvious that it was time for me to grow up and realize that He had work for me to do which would require my total trust and confidence in Him.

Without the threat of losing Robert and all these things in my life, I would have never experienced this new perspective. He taught me that wherever I find myself in life, if I am diligently seeking Him, He will direct me. He will place me exactly where He wants so I can be used by Him to accomplish His purpose. I now trust God daily to provide and sustain me with *everything* I need. In return, He pours His blessings out on me and my family.

> "For I know the thoughts and plans that I have for you, says the Lord, thoughts and plans for welfare and peace and not for evil, to give you hope in your final outcome. Then you will call upon Me, and you will come and pray to Me, and I will hear and heed you. Then you will seek Me, inquire for, and require Me [as a vital necessity] and find Me when you search for Me with all your heart. I will be found by you, says the Lord, and I will release you from captivity and gather you from all the nations and all the places to which I have driven you, says the Lord, and I will bring you back to the place from which I caused you to be carried away captive" (Jeremiah 29:11–14, AMP).

As you well know by now, I love this passage—especially the last verse. It is a promise from God that I have counted on from the very beginning of this whole experience. From the very beginning I felt that Robert and I had been carried away as captives from our lives, and I trusted that God would bring us back—just as He promised.

Thanks to God and His mercy, He has given more of our lives back to us now. We are only in the doctor's office every six weeks for a couple of hours, and we get to return to our wonderful life. I have a totally new respect for my life and my family. I appreciate every day that God gives us, and I live a much more thankful life.

My goal is to try to never allow a change of plans, problem, or disagreement with someone to consume my day. I try to resolve the problem and adjust to the change as quickly as possible so I don't waste even a minute of my life. Life is a precious gift, and the special people in our lives are blessings from God. I never want to take for granted the gifts God has given me ever again.

We walk by faith, and we will not weaken our faith when we consider Robert's blood counts, which are weakened by aplastic anemia. No unbelief or distrust will make us waver concerning the promise of God. We grow strong and are empowered by faith as we give praise and glory to God. We are fully satisfied and assured that God is able and mighty to keep His Word and to do what He has promised.

As I write this, I am reminded by God through my daily devotion in *Streams in the Dessert*:

> "True faith relies on God and believes before seeing. Naturally we want some evidence that our petition is granted before we believe, but when we 'live by faith' (2 Corinthians 5:7), we need no evidence other than God's Word. He has spoken, and in harmony with our faith it will be done. We will see because we have believed, and true faith sustains us in the most trying of times, even when everything around us seems to contradict God's Word… Faith that believes it will see, will keep us from becoming discouraged. We will laugh at seemingly impossible situations while we watch with

delight to see how God is going to open a path through our Red Sea. It is in these places of severe testing, with no human way out of our difficulty, that our faith grows and is strengthened."[3]

Become Childlike

It has been amazing to watch Robert as he has faced this disease. He has been courageous and has truly allowed God to take something that the enemy intended for his harm and turn it into good. Witnessing Robert as he faced and dealt with this disease has been an eye-opening experience for me, and his attitude has been remarkable. God has used him to teach me so much through this experience. From the first day at the hospital, it was as if I was witnessing the face of a child. Robert's childlike faith has been incredible! There was no doubt that he knew his Father would take care of him.

In Mark 10:15 Jesus tells us, "Truly I tell you, whoever does not receive and accept and welcome the kingdom of God like a little child [does] positively shall not enter it at all" (AMP).

A child's perspective is very different than an adult's in so many ways. Have you ever taken the time to witness a child's demeanor on an average day? Why do they (for the most part) seem so happy and content living in the moment? The present is their only perspective, and their faces and attitudes directly reflect their simplicity.

One Sunday morning, I was sitting at church, admiring a couple of my favorite young friends playing as they waited patiently for their parents after the service. As I watched these two, I was very intrigued by how happy and carefree they were as they talked and laughed together. Their faces were animated as they danced around with the freedom to express themselves, and I found them quite entertaining as I watched in anticipation of their every move.

Suddenly, I felt in my spirit that God was trying to get my attention. He had used these children to catch my eye on purpose. He was trying to express to me that these children were the perfect example of what He wants for me. He wants me to enjoy each day—just like these children playing in front of me.

As I considered the attitudes of these children, I began to think about their perspective. Why were they so happy, carefree, and full of energy?

These children were blessed with great parents and were very well provided for. They were living only for the moment and enjoying life. Could the smiles on their faces be evidence that they trusted their parents to provide and take care of them? Could it be that they felt safe and secure, knowing their parents were not only there beside them, but also watching over them?

They also seemed very relaxed and content with—not only each other, but also themselves. They were completely comfortable being the children that God created, and they seemed to have no desire to be anything but themselves.

Theses children were obviously very content just spending time laughing and living with complete faith in their parents. What a gift to live with a faith that is altered by nothing.

I then felt in my spirit that this attitude of faith is exactly what God wants for me—and all His children. This was truly a great example of how the children of God should live.

We should carry the confidence and freedom of a child, knowing that our Father is with us and watching over us. We should be happy with who we are in Christ and be confident in Him! We should enjoy being the person God created. We should feel safe and secure knowing that if we are looking to Him, He will take care and provide for us no matter what. God wants what's best for us. I was touched and deeply moved by the love of God during this experience. God is good!

I was reading a devotional from *Streams in the Desert* one morning, and I ran across this story. I think that this is the perfect example of childlike faith:

"Whatever you ask for in prayer, believe that you have received it, and it will be yours" (Mark 11:24, NIV).

When my little son was about ten years old, his grandmother promised him a stamp collecting album for Christmas. Christmas came and went with no stamp album and no word from Grandma. The matter, however, was not mentioned, until his friends came to see his Christmas presents. I was astonished, after he had listed all the gifts he had received, to hear him add, "And a stamp album from my grandmother."

After hearing this several times, I called my son to me and said, "But George, you didn't get a stamp album from Grandma. Why did you say you did?"

With a puzzled look on his face, as if I had asked a very strange question, he replied, "Well, Mom, Grandma *said*, and that is the *same as*." Not a word from me would sway his faith.

A month passed, and nothing else was said about the album. Finally one day, to test his faith and because I wondered in my own heart why the album had not been sent, I said, "George, I think Grandma has forgotten her promise."

"Oh no, Mom," he quickly and firmly responded. "She hasn't."

I watched his sweet, trusting face, which for a while looked very serious, as if he were debating the possibility I had suggested. Soon his face brightened as he said, "Do you think it would do any good for me to write Grandma, *thanking* her for the album?"

"I don't know," I said, "but you might try it." A rich spiritual truth then began to dawn on me.

> In a few minutes, a letter was written and mailed, as George went off whistling his confidence in his grandma. Soon a letter from Grandma arrived with this message:
>
> My dear George,
>
> I have not forgotten my promise to you for a stamp album. I could not find the one you wanted here, so I ordered one from New York. It did not arrive until after Christmas, and it was not the right one. I then ordered another, but it still has not arrived. I have decided to send you thirty dollars instead so that you may buy the one you want in Chicago.
>
> Your loving Grandma.
>
> As he read the letter, his face was the face of a victor. From the depths of a heart that never doubted came the words, "Now, Mom, didn't I tell you?" George "against all hope … in hope believed" (Romans 4:18) that the stamp album would come. And while he was trusting, Grandma was working, and in due time faith became sight.
>
> It is only human to want to see before we step out on the promises of God. Yet our Savior said to Thomas and to a long list of doubters who have followed, "Blessed are those who have not seen and yet have believed" (John 20:29).[1]

Wow—to have the faith of this little boy—the faith of a child! Jesus said in Matthew 19:14, "Let the little children come to me, and do not hinder them, for the kingdom of heaven belongs to such as these" (NIV).

~

Soon after my dad went to heaven, our dog escaped from the radio fence in our backyard and was struck and immediately killed by a car in the busy road below us. Lynn was an absolutely beautiful, energetic, full-bred border collie. She was my daughter's pride and joy. It was very hard to lose her—especially that soon after my dad's death.

We were actually preparing to move back to our hometown at the time, and we knew that finding another dog for our daughter wasn't a very good idea until we were settled in our new home. However, my daughter had different ideas. She started praying every night at bedtime for a new puppy. She actually asked me to pray with her for that special little puppy. As I reluctantly prayed with her every night, I knew in my heart that this just wasn't the right time to find another dog.

Very soon after we began praying for that special little puppy, we got a knock at our door. I opened my door to a neighbor I had never met who lived up the street. He greeted me and explained that he had seen our dog in the road, and he offered his condolences. He then began to share that he had been driving down the interstate and noticed a very tiny puppy on the side of the road. He continued to explain that after he picked the puppy up, he immediately thought of our family and wondered if we would be interested in giving the little stray a home.

I asked him if he had any idea of what breed of dog the puppy was, and without hesitation, he responded by saying that she was a Chihuahua. I began to explain to him that ever since I was a very young child, I had wanted a Chihuahua. Due to an allergy to dogs, I could not have one inside the house. Imagine my surprise when he then told me about his mother who had the same problem and owned two Chihuahuas. He then began to explain that she provided her dogs a bed warmer in the cold months, and her Chihuahuas were perfectly happy and healthy living outside.

I'll never forget stepping out to his truck and seeing the puppy for the first time. She was so tiny and absolutely covered with fleas and ticks. It was love at first sight! My daughter named her Maya. She is straight from heaven and is a blessing to my family. She is an amazing dog and has never been any trouble. She is now about ten years old and has proven to be that special little puppy my daughter earnestly prayed for. Not only did God deliver her puppy to our door, but he also gave me a desire of my heart that I thought was never possible.

God is our amazing Father, and we should trust Him and count on Him for our every need with His perfect timing. Let me remind you of the words from Mark 11:24: "Therefore I tell you, whatever you ask for in prayer, believe that you have received it, and it will be yours" (NIV).

Just like these children with simple, childlike faith, we have asked God to heal Robert. We take Him at His Word and are already thanking Him for our answered prayer. We count on God to do as He has promised. We don't focus on our circumstances, but on God's promises. We speak and pray His promises and eagerly wait to see what He does next. We anticipate how He will direct and open our path through this disease.

The Lord declares in Jeremiah 30:17, "I will restore you to health and heal your wounds" (NIV). "God, who does not lie, promised" (Titus 1:2, NIV).

I am once again reminded through my daily devotional from *Streams in the Desert:*

> "Faith is not conjuring up, through an act of your will, a sense of certainty that something is going to happen. No, it is recognizing God's promise as an actual fact, believing it is true, rejoicing in the knowledge of that truth, and then simply resting because God said it. Faith turns a promise into a prophecy. A promise is contingent upon our cooperation, but when we exercise genuine faith in it, it becomes a prophecy. Then we can move ahead with certainty that it will come to pass, because 'God … does not lie'"[2]
>
> "Have faith in God [constantly]" (Mark 11:22, AMP).

A Sling and a Stone

When my family was faced with aplastic anemia, the Word of God literally saved us. Without God and His Word, I honestly don't know how we would have survived—especially during those first few months. Listening to His Word was like being thrown a life preserver. My family has stood on His promises, and they have not let us down. I can proudly say that God and His promises are the reason my family and I are the happiest we have ever been in our lives.

You can count on God's Word. God loves you! You are His child, and He would never make promises to you that He would not keep. He will never break a promise to you or let you down.

God has made us many promises, and the Bible is absolutely full of them. The Word tells us in Psalm 37:3–7: "Trust in the LORD and do good; dwell in the land and enjoy safe pasture. Delight yourself in the LORD and he will give you the desires of your heart. Commit your way to the LORD; trust in him and he will do this: He will make your righteousness shine like the dawn, the justice of your cause like the noonday sun. Be still before the LORD and wait patiently for him" (NIV).

As I have experienced God these past few years, I have gained a totally new respect for His Word. A few years ago, I went to a Bible exhibit, and it was there that I came to a better understanding of the history of the Bible. I highly recommend going to one of these exhibits if you ever get the chance. I wasn't aware that so many people have given up their lives to save God's Word from being destroyed. When you learn more about the Bible's history, you become more aware of how blessed we are to have it. Over the last few years, as Robert and I have relied on God's Word so completely, I feel that God has given me an even better understanding of why the enemy has tried so hard to destroy it. But before I share that, let's look at one of my favorite promises. It is Matthew 17:20: "I tell you the truth, if you have faith as small as a mustard seed, you can say to this mountain, 'Move from here to there' and it will move. Nothing will be impossible for you" (NIV).

As I read these verses one morning during my prayer time, I thought to myself, "I would really like to see a mustard seed." From that day on, I was determined to buy some seeds at my next visit to the grocery store. This went on for many weeks without success. I somehow could not remember to buy the seeds at the appropriate time.

One Sunday morning, I gave a testimony at my church, and a very sweet friend came over to me after the service and handed me a tiny glass jar. The tiny jar contained none other than one single mustard seed. She then began to explain that she had actually bought it for someone else, but after my witness, she felt compelled to give it to me. I was blown away—not only by the fact that God had led her to buy, bring, and then give the seed to me, but also by the fact that this was a desire of my heart. It had only crossed my mind and hadn't been mentioned to anyone. The fact that God had led someone to go to all that trouble for me blew me away. God is so sweet.

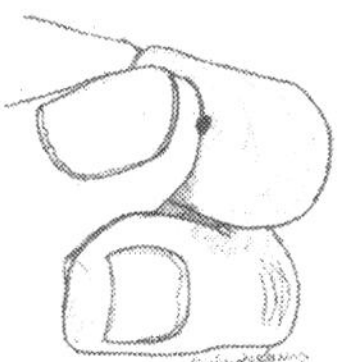

I think that sometimes it does us good to be reminded of just how small a mustard seed is. Do you really comprehend what this verse is saying? If we have faith the size of one of the smallest seeds in the world, then we can speak to the mountain, and it will move. Nothing will be impossible for us. Wow!

Several years ago, I read an incredible book by Jim Cymbala called *Fresh Faith.* I highly recommend reading this book. Let's look at a couple great quotes from the book:

> "The promises of God are appropriated only by faith."[1]

> "We receive things, even the things God has promised us, only if we have faith."[2]

~

I now want to take you to a couple accounts in history through God's Word that I believe have been given to us to set examples of how we should face the battles in our lives. Let's start with the promise from Joshua 23. In Joshua 23:14, the Word says, "You know with all your heart and soul that not one of all the good promises the LORD your God gave you has failed. Every promise has been fulfilled; not one has failed" (NIV).

Considering who Joshua was and all that he witnessed and experienced throughout his life, these are some very strong words. If you are unfamiliar with the lives of Joshua and Caleb, I encourage you to read the book of Numbers. If you are interested in learning more about their lives, the intriguing part starts in Numbers 13.

Because of their faith in God, Joshua and Caleb were the only two out of the original group of Israelites to actually enter the Promised Land. That original group consisted of around 600,000 men—that's not even counting the women and children.

We love this story and believe that the pivotal moment for them was when Moses sent the spies across the Jordan River into the Promised Land to check it out. All but two came back with a negative report. The majority of them said that the land was filled with giants and there was no way that they would be able to overtake the giants. Joshua and Caleb were the only two spies who came back with a positive report. It was their faith that allowed them to encourage the others and report that they could overtake the enemy, because the Lord would be with them.

The second account is the story of David, which is found in 1 Samuel 17. David set a great example of how we should deal with our battles. The Israelites were up against the giant, Goliath, and David, a young shepherd who had only been sent to deliver a package to his brothers, wanted to fight the giant.

The Word tells us in 1 Samuel 17:34-37: "David said to Saul, 'Your servant has been keeping his father's sheep. When a lion or a bear came and carried off a sheep from the flock, I went after it, struck it and rescued the sheep from its mouth. When it turned on me, I seized it by its hair, struck it and killed it. Your servant has killed both the lion and the bear; this uncircumcised Philistine will be like one of them, because he has defied the armies of the living God. The LORD who delivered me from the paw of the lion and the paw of the bear will deliver me from the hand of this Philistine.' Saul said to David, 'Go, and the LORD be with you'" (NIV).

As you can see, David had amazing faith in God. Let's look at 1 Samuel 17:45–50. This is my favorite part:

> "Then David said to the Philistine, 'You come to me with a sword, with a spear, and with a javelin. But I come to you in the name of the LORD of hosts, the God of the armies of Israel, whom you have defied. This day the LORD will deliver you into my hand, and I will strike you and take your head from you. And this day I will give the carcasses of the camp of the Philistines to the birds of the air and the wild beasts of the earth, that all the earth may know that there is a God in Israel. Then all this assembly shall know that the LORD does not save with sword and spear; for the battle *is* the LORD's, and He will give you into our hands.'
>
> So it was, when the Philistine arose and came and drew near to meet David, that David hurried and ran toward the army to meet the Philistine. Then David put his hand in his bag and took out a stone; and he slung *it* and struck the Philistine in his forehead, so that the stone sank into his forehead, and he fell on his face to

> the earth. So David prevailed over the Philistine with a sling and a stone, and struck the Philistine and killed him. But *there was* no sword in the hand of David" (NKJV).

Notice that as David prepared for the battle, he proclaimed what was going to happen. He declared what the Lord would do. I love this verse. David put his faith into action with a sling and one small stone.

Robert and I recently received a gift from one of our special friends from our church family. It was a sling and five smooth stones. We were told by this person that during his prayer time one day, he was led to make the sling and collect the stones. He spent one whole afternoon walking through the river, hunting the perfect stones. As I share this sweet experience, I can't help but think of 1 Samuel 17:40: "Then he took his staff in his hand, chose five smooth stones from the stream, put them in the pouch of his shepherd's bag and, with his sling in his hand, approached the Philistine" (NIV).

Our friend shared with us that at first he wasn't even sure what he was supposed to do with the sling and stones, but then God led him to give them to Robert. Isn't that amazing? God is awesome, and we have some precious, obedient friends.

When you hold the sling and stones in your hands, you come to a serious realization of just how amazing David's actions really were. David killed a man nearly ten feet tall with only a small stone. He had his weapon and ammunition in his possession, but without his faith, he would have been killed. By putting his faith into action, God gave him supernatural power to kill the giant with one small stone.

One of the many reasons I love this account of David is because it reminds me so much of Robert. When Robert was faced with his giant (this disease), he put his faith into action. Just like David, he proclaimed what was going to happen and declared what God would do.

Robert has always been a very positive person—so much so that it has really annoyed me in the past. I just wasn't a believer that speaking positively over your situation would change anything. Don't get me wrong, I wasn't a really negative person, but I just didn't believe that you could change anything by speaking positive words. Well, I am now a believer! He approached this disease with a completely positive attitude, and I have personally witnessed that the positive words make a difference. During our stay at the hospital, a couple of nurses even commented that their positive-speaking patients always seem to have fewer side affects and recover more quickly than those who speak negatively.

I now realize that this is what God's Word teaches us in Proverbs 18:21: "Death and life are in the power of the tongue, and they who indulge in it shall eat the fruit of it [for death or life]" (AMP). I now understand this verse much better.

I hope you agree with me in saying that Joshua, Caleb, and David are all great examples of how we can rely on God in our battles. These are accounts of people having faith in God and putting their faith into action! Without their faith, Joshua and Caleb would have never entered the Promise Land, and David would have never defeated the giant. When they showed God that they trusted Him and took Him at His word, God took care of them and blessed them.

There are many children of God in the Bible with awesome faith stories. I wish I could share more.

In 2 Corinthians 5:7, the Word tells us to "live by faith and not by sight" (NIV). In Hebrews 11:6, we are also told, "without faith it is impossible to please God" (NIV). If faith pleases God, how do we do this? How do we live this way?

What exactly is Faith? The *American Heritage Dictionary* defines faith as "confident belief; trust".[3]

1 John 5:4 tells us, "The conquering power that brings the world to its knees is our faith. The person who wins out over the world's ways is simply the one who believes Jesus is the Son of God" *(The Message).*

In Hebrews 11:1, the Word says, "Now faith is being sure of what we hope for and certain of what we do not see" (NIV). It also tells us in Hebrews 11:3, "By faith we understand that the universe was formed at God's command, so that what is seen was not made out of what was visible" (NIV).

How do we obtain this type of faith—the type of faith that Joshua, Caleb, and David had? I think you would agree with me in saying that we all want this kind of faith. We all want our faith to grow.

I once heard a minister teach about how to grow faith, and I thought it was a pretty interesting example.

If we want to grow something, we most certainly need a seed. In the Bible, one of the parables Jesus used referred to God's Word as seed. Mark 4:14 says, "The farmer sows the word" (NIV). If God's Word is a seed, then we can easily say that God has provided us with a variety of seeds for anything we could ever need.

What does God's Word tell us about how to grow faith? In Romans 10:17, the Word tells us, "So then faith cometh by hearing, and hearing by the word of God" (KJV).

A seed has to be planted in soil to grow. The Word of God is very similar, only it needs to be planted in our hearts. How is the Word of God planted in our hearts? Our faith grows by hearing the Word, so we allow the Holy Spirit to plant and grow these seeds in our hearts by speaking or praying God's Word out loud.

After a seed is planted, it needs to be nurtured to grow and produce. It needs lots of water, and the weeds need to be regularly pulled. The Word is no different. Not only does the Word or seed of faith need to be spoken throughout each day, but it needs watered regularly with praise and thanksgiving. We also need to keep away any weeds of doubt by refusing to dwell on negative thoughts. As those thoughts, or weeds, surface, we should replace them by meditating on the verses.

As you wait for a seed to produce, you can envision it in your mind as you count on it meeting your expectations. Thank God for answered prayers before you receive them, and enjoy this time waiting in total confidence.

We have established that faith comes from hearing the Word of God. Wouldn't we then have to assume that the Word of God contains power?

John 1:1 says, "In the beginning was the Word, and the Word was with God, and the Word was God" (NIV).

In Luke 4:32, we are told, "they were astonished at His doctrine: for His Word was with power" (KJV).

Psalm 138:2 says, "I will worship toward Your holy temple and praise Your name for Your loving-kindness and for Your truth and faithfulness; for You have exalted above all else Your name and Your word and You have magnified Your word above all Your name!" (AMP) This verse tells us that God's Word is magnified above even His name! If the Word is above even His name, then it is extremely powerful. The next question is, where does the power come from if it is spoken and heard?

In John 14:15–17, the Word says, "If you love me, you will obey what I command. And I will ask the Father, and he will give you another Counselor to be with you forever the Spirit of truth. The world cannot accept him, because it neither sees him nor knows him. But you know him, for he lives with you and will be in you" (NIV).

If the Holy Spirit lives inside of us and we speak the Word of God, does that mean the Spirit of God is using our voice to speak His Words? If he can use our hands and feet, can He also use our voices? Is it possible to appropriate God's promises by speaking God's Holy Word out of our mouths through prayer?

I'll never forget the night Robert and I attended a prayer service at our church the evening after September 11. My family, like most everyone, felt quite anxious and a bit uneasy the first few days following the attack. I will always remember when our pastor read verses from the Psalms during that service and how powerful the Word seemed. I felt God's presence strongly as he read the verses. I was so comforted by God's Word, and the power I felt really got my attention that night.

This is one of my favorite quotes by Jim Cymbala from the book *Fresh Faith:*

> "God is looking for a people who will believe Him and take Him at His Word no matter what the circumstances say or what other people are telling us."[4]

~

Years ago, I heard someone say that they had prayed the prayer of Jabez, and the person saw God do great things. At that time in my life, I felt that I had nothing to lose, so I started reading that prayer several times a day. I printed the prayer on a small piece of paper and placed it in my windowsill over the kitchen sink. As I cleaned up the dishes throughout each day, I would pray the prayer—sometimes silently, and sometimes out loud. At the time I started this prayer, my husband was working for a company he had been employed with for seventeen years. Although he had provided very well for our family throughout the years, his job was very stressful for both of us. Our finances were up and down, and we seemed to just get by.

Some time later, I discovered that the prayer of Jabez was actually a verse from the Bible. I was not aware of this at the time I started reading the prayer. The verses are from 1 Chronicles 4:10, "And Jabez called on the God of Israel saying, 'Oh, that you would bless me indeed, and enlarge my territory, that Your hand would be with me and that You would keep me from evil, that I may not cause pain'" (NKJV).

In very little time, God started moving in my family in a big way. We were not serious about tithing at the time that I started the prayer. Our income was based on commission, so we would tithe when our income was good, but would always stop giving when our income went down and business was bad. Sometime after I started speaking the verse, we began to feel led to step out in faith and seriously tithe—no matter what our bank account looked like.

When we stepped out in obedience with total trust in God and tithed, He absolutely blew us away with His provision. When we began giving, we knew that we wouldn't have enough money to get us through the month, but we decided that we would just trust God and be obedient. Every month, God provided everything that we needed to get through financially. We received unexpected checks in the mail that were exactly the amount we needed. It was amazing, and we were blessed by seeing the Lord work through other people and unexpected places. We made it through each month with every bill paid and everything that we needed. God is very creative, and He is faithful! He never let us down.

It required a lot of faith to be obedient with an income based on commissions, and it was way out of our comfort zone. As I reflect back on this time in our lives, I now realize where that faith came from. I believe that as I spoke God's Word, my faith grew and gave me the courage to step out and be obedient. At the time, I was clueless and had no concept of the power of God's Word.

I was soon given a great idea that would require me to step out of my comfort zone once again and start a career. I had been a homemaker for years, staying home to raise my daughter. This career would require me to further my education and acquire several licenses. This was something I had dreamed about for many years. I now know that this idea came from God, and He gave me a desire of my heart. I spent several years working with my husband, and our territory was enlarged—almost double—as was our income.

Although we no longer felt completely comfortable with the direction that our company was moving, we were very thankful for the many years of employment. Before long my husband was led through a close friend to apply for a different position with another company. Within several months, Robert was offered a position with this company, and after nineteen years of employment, he accepted the job. He now works for a wonderful company whose mission statement is based on the Word of God. His prospects are endless, and he absolutely loves his job. Yes, God answered my prayer of Jabez.

All throughout the Bible, we are reminded time and time again that God's Word is powerful. With His words, He created the universe and everything in it. In Genesis 1:3, we are told that God said, "Let there be light; and there was light" (KJV). God *said!* His words produced the power that created the light!

I challenge you with whatever issue or problem you might be experiencing in your life to open the Bible and allow the Lord to lead you to a verse or promise that pertains to your problem or need. Allow God to grow your faith by speaking or praying the verse or verses out loud several times a day. Maybe you need courage, strength, or encouragement to accomplish a project. Maybe you are dealing with fear and anxiety. You might need healing, or maybe you just need wisdom for a decision you must make. Nothing is too big or too small for God!

Spend time praising God and thanking Him for what He will do. Keep your eyes open. Expectantly watch where and how He will be at work in your life. As you do this God will move in a mighty way as He grows and blossoms your seeds of faith.

> "I am the LORD, the God of all mankind. Is anything too hard for me?" (Jeremiah 32:27, NIV)

Pleading the Promises

My daughter is an animal lover, and we have tried to accommodate her affections by owning many different animals throughout her childhood. In her younger years, almost every summer, we raised a duckling or two. If they hadn't flown away by late fall, then we would set them free at the lake near her grandparents' home. Throughout the years and our experiences with the ducks, we have acquired quite a few stories and have become very familiar with ducks' mannerisms. We actually had to perform several ducky funerals from completely innocent accidents with our dog and the unexpected steps of our daughter.

The fatalities were random, and one actually took place one morning while my daughter was playing on the patio when she was around three or four years old. Her duck's name was Scooter, and he was so accustomed to following her every step that when she changed directions, he ended up under her foot. We laid Scooter to rest that afternoon.

We also performed another ducky funeral several years later when we had shown a little too much confidence in our beagle, Ginger. We stepped away for just a couple of minutes, and the poor teenage duck was mortally wounded. After doing all that we could to save him, the little guy expired.

We trained Ginger to respect and live in harmony with many of our ducky friends. Ginger even shared her doghouse with one particular duck. They grew to be very close friends, and they snuggled up together every night.

About five years ago, my daughter burst through the back door of our home with tears streaming down her face. As she caught her breath, she began to explain that while cleaning out the duck pen, her little duckling friend had run up behind her without her knowledge. As she turned around, she accidentally stepped on him. She then proceeded to explain that she thought she had stepped on his head and neck, and her whole weight was on him for a brief moment. As she continued to cry, she explained that she didn't think he had a chance of surviving.

Before I continue with this story, I should describe the type of day we had before this episode. It was one of those days in your life which you will always remember but so badly want to forget. We were in the middle of a family crisis, and we were truly struggling to get through the day. We were assisting a couple of our family members in a serious and messy situation. I was about at the end of my rope.

We immediately ran out to our little friend and assessed his injury. It wasn't good. He struggled to keep his head up with no success, and his breathing was labored. We began to have flashbacks. After witnessing the previous two duckling deaths, it was obvious to both my husband and I that he wasn't going to make it.

In my desperation, I turned to God, knowing that I didn't have the energy or mindset to deal with counseling another emotionally distressed member of my family on this particular day. I laid my hand on the duck and silently but boldly prayed for God to heal the little guy. As I prayed over our little friend, I felt God's presence very strongly. Little did I know Robert was praying at this same time. Neither of us mentioned praying over the duck until later that evening.

Within just a few minutes, the little duck began to successfully hold his head up, and within a few more minutes, his breathing improved. By the end of the day, he was walking around and doing very well. For a few weeks, he was unable to open one eye, but after those few weeks, he was as good as new.

Later that evening, as we discussed the day's events, Robert shared that as he prayed for God to heal the duck, he also experienced God's presence in a very strong way. We are convinced that God healed the duck.

When Robert was diagnosed with aplastic anemia, our lives were turned upside down. Although God led us to a great doctor and Robert received the best treatment possible, we knew that God had the ultimate control over our life. We had a crisis of belief. We had to decide whether we were going to believe the promises of God's Word or not. We chose to believe God's promises, and we knew that we had to get God involved in Robert's healing. I shared this last experience with you to help you understand that when Robert was diagnosed, we both knew from the very beginning that God could heal him. After experiencing God's healing power with the little duck in our backyard that summer afternoon, we knew that He could certainly heal Robert.

There are so many accounts in the Bible of people receiving healing that I felt I should focus my attention on what the Bible had to say about the subject. Through my study, God led me to many different verses in His Word and sources of information through several other books. All of my findings pointed to one common theme—God's Word.

These next few verses really got my attention. In Matthew 8:16, the Word tells us, "They brought unto him many that were possessed with devils: and he cast out the spirits with his word, and healed all that were sick" (KJV). The Bible actually says that Jesus healed the sick with His words.

In Joel 2:11, the Word says, "And the LORD shall utter his voice before his army: for his camp is very great: for he is strong that executeth his Word" (KJV).

Psalm 103:20 says, "Bless the LORD, ye his angels, that excel in strength, that do his commandments, hearkening unto the voice of his Word" (KJV).

Not only did my research conclude that God's Word contains power, but I found that speaking or praying His Word out loud builds faith and connects us to the Father in a mighty way.

In Ezekiel 37:4, 7, 10, the Word says, "Again he said unto me, 'Prophesy upon these bones, and say unto them, O ye dry bones, hear the Word of the Lord.' So I prophesied as I was commanded: and as I prophesied, there was a noise, and behold a shaking, and the bones came together, bone to his bone. So I prophesied as he commanded me, and the breath came into them, and they lived, and stood up upon their feet, an exceeding great army" (KJV).

These are just a few of the many examples made available to us in the Bible that teach us about the power of speaking God's Word.

However, I must point out that the act of simply speaking God's Word will not automatically cause change in your life. We must *first believe* in God and His promises. If you find it difficult to believe or struggle with your faith, I want to remind you of these words from Romans 12:3: "God has dealt to each one a measure of faith" (NKJV).

I must also remind you that the Holy Spirit is the one that works through us—it's not our voice alone. And most importantly, we must recognize that the will of the Father is decided by the Father alone. As we read, believe, and speak the scriptures, the Holy Spirit demonstrates the power of God's Word in our lives according to the will of the Father and according to His purpose. Paul speaks of this in 1 Corinthians 12:7, "Now to each one the manifestation of the Spirit is given for the common good" (NIV).

After God led me through several days of research, I understood just what we needed to do. We selected a few healing scriptures and began to speak and pray them out loud several times a day. Robert prays the verses regularly every day, just like he takes his prescription medication. We have been speaking and praying God's healing words over Robert ever since.

"Remember Your Word to Your servant, for You have given me hope" (Psalm 119:49, NIV).

Last year, I picked up a book in my closet that had been there for several years. I had once ordered a set of tapes from a minister on television, and the book was an added gift sent with the tapes. I wasn't interested in reading it, so I placed it on the shelf in my closet. I thought about giving it away several times, but I never did. One day, as I was cleaning out my closet, I ran across the book. For some reason, I decided that I should read it. The book is Joel Osteen's *Your Best Life Now.*

I don't believe that the book just happened to be in my closet or I just happened to pick it up and read it at this particular time. I believe that God went before me and placed the book in my possession Himself, because it was His intention for me to read it at this appointed time.

In the book, Joel talks about his mother, who was diagnosed with metastatic cancer of the liver. She was told that she had approximately two weeks to live and was basically sent home to die. Joel reminded me in the book: "We serve a supernatural God. He is not limited to the laws of nature. He can do what human beings cannot do. He can make a way in our lives where it looks as if there is no way."[1]

Osteen also explained that when his mother arrived home, she began speaking God's words of healing throughout each day. As each month passed, she began to feel better and slowly but surely, she regained her strength. Year after year, she improved. She is alive and cancer-free twenty years later! Isn't that amazing?

I felt like God was encouraging us with this story. He wanted us to keep it up. Joel's mother wasn't healed overnight, but little by little. We continue to speak and pray God's words every day, and we believe that God will keep His promises. Robert is doing very well.

~

> "He is the God of limitless resources—the only limit comes from us. Our requests, our thoughts, and our prayers are too small, and our expectations are too low. God is trying to raise our vision to a higher level, call us to have greater expectations, and thereby bring us to greater appropriation. Shall we continue living in a way that mocks His will and denies His Word?
>
> There is no limit to what we may ask and expect of our glorious El Shaddai—our almighty God. And there is no way for us to measure His blessing, for He is 'able to do immeasurably more than all we ask or imagine, according to his power that is at work within us' (Ephesians 3:20).

> The way to find God's treasure-house of blessing is to climb the ladder of His divine promises. Those promises are the key that opens the door to the riches of God's grace and favor" (L. B. Cowman, *Streams in the Desert).*[2]

~

Getting back to the history of the Bible, I believe the enemy knows the Word of God is true and it contains power! This is the reason the enemy has worked so hard to destroy God's Word through the ages. By the way, the Bible is still the best-selling book ever written. Shouldn't that get our attention?

Have you ever heard someone say that they don't believe everything that they read in the Bible because it was written by man? Isn't it interesting that you never hear anyone say that about history books?

Have you ever wondered why it is that when we read history books, we never doubt the information, but when we read the stories in the Bible, we are sometimes tempted to doubt them?

History books and the Bible were both written by man. What is the difference? Consider this for a minute. Both history books and the Bible were written by people giving accounts of events that took place in the past. The main difference in the two is that the Bible was God-inspired.

In 2 Timothy 3:16–17, the Word tells us, "All Scripture is given by inspiration of God, and is profitable for doctrine, for reproof, for correction, for instruction in righteousness, that the man of God may be complete, thoroughly equipped for every good work" (NKJV).

It also tells us in 2 Peter 1:21, "No prophecy ever originated because some man willed it [to do so—it never came by human impulse], but men spoke from God who were borne along (moved and impelled) by the Holy Spirit" (AMP).

Have you ever wondered why some people have no problem believing that Jesus died on the cross for them, but do have trouble believing other stories and verses in the Bible? How can they believe some of the Bible but not all of it?

Again, I believe the enemy knows that the Word of God is true and there is power in the Word. This is why he tempts us to doubt and works so hard to keep us from the truth. The Word actually warns us of this in Mark 4:15: "Some people are like seed along the path, where the word is sown. As soon as they hear it, Satan comes and takes away the word that was sown in them" (NIV).

Just like most everyone, I have negative thoughts cross my mind from time to time tempting me to doubt God and His Word. For years, when these negative thoughts crossed my mind, I was riddled with guilt. I somehow felt responsible for the actual thoughts which were tempting me. I now know that these destructive thoughts are from the enemy. I also understand that guilt is not from God, because the Word teaches in Romans 8:1: "Therefore, there is now no condemnation for those who are in Christ Jesus" (NIV). It is unbelievable how much guilt and condemnation that I have experienced over the years through this deceit. I have fallen for this all my life.

I realize that some would argue this point and suggest that these destructive thoughts are a result of what remains of our sinful nature. The Word does tell us in Galatians 5:17, "For the flesh desires what is contrary to the Spirit, and the Spirit what is contrary to the flesh" (NIV). Although I am certainly no expert on this subject, I do understand that after accepting Christ into our hearts we receive a new nature and our old nature or flesh does oppose our new nature. However, isn't the enemy entrenched within our old sinful nature? Aren't Satan and our flesh at war against us? In my opinion, no matter which way you look at it, negative, destructive thought patterns originate from the enemy and everyone battles against them.

The Bible is God-inspired and alive, and I happen to believe that God's Word has been given to help us in these battles. The Bible is a gift from God, and we should absolutely celebrate the honor of owning a copy.

I am thankful for His Word and for seeing and understanding the truth! This truth is setting me free from the bondage that has kept me from God's best for my life. The Word tells us to hold to His teaching, and we "will know the truth and the truth will set [us] free" (John 8:31–32, NIV).

Keep in mind that if the Word of God is just left in the book and not utilized by us, then our lives will lack faith and purpose. Utilizing God's words and seeing Him become active in our lives is essential to enjoying and living the wonderful life that Jesus died for us to have.

The Bible tells us in Hebrews 4:12 that "the Word of God is living and active. Sharper than any double-edged sword, it penetrates even to dividing soul and spirit" (NIV). This same verse from the Amplified Bible says, "For the Word that God speaks is alive and full of power [making it active, operative, energizing, and effective]; it is sharper than any two-edged sword, penetrating to the dividing line of the breath of life (soul) and [the immortal] spirit."

As you hold your Bible in your hands, you hold powerful ammunition for your defense against the enemy. God promises that if you have a relationship with Him, the Holy Spirit will live inside you. When you speak God's Word, your faith *will* grow, and you *will* experience God in your life.

We can find reassurance in the words from Isaiah 51:15–16: "For I am the Lord your God, Who stirs up the sea so that its waves roar and Who by rebuke restrains it—the Lord of hosts is His name. And I have put My words in your mouth and have covered you with the shadow of My hand" (AMP). Interestingly enough, these last few words from the Lord are also spoken in Jeremiah 1:9: "And the Lord said to me, 'Behold, I have put My words in your mouth'" (AMP). In Jeremiah 1:12, the Lord promises: "I am alert and active, watching over My Word to perform it" (AMP).

As I mentioned before, David held the sling and stones, and he put his faith into action. With the help of the Lord, he killed the giant. I believe that just like David, Robert is putting his faith into action, and God will supernaturally heal him.

"For nothing will be impossible with God" (Luke 1:37, NASB).

I once again challenge you to put your faith into action and allow God to grow your faith by watering your life and circumstances with God's Word. Be prepared to be amazed. "Then you will call, and the LORD will answer; you will cry for help, and He will say: Here am I" (Isaiah 58:9, NIV).

"The one who calls you is faithful and He will do it" (1 Thessalonians 5:24, NIV).

Keep in mind that you must be willing to totally trust Him and accept that He won't always move in your life and your circumstances in the way you might desire or expect. He is your Father, and He knows what is best for His children. Speaking or praying God's Word is not a way to satisfy your own worldly desires, but rather a way to align your life with the will of the Father.

"Roll your works upon the Lord [commit and trust them wholly to Him; He will cause your thoughts to become agreeable to His will, and] so shall your plans be established and succeed" (Proverbs 16:3, AMP).

There will be times when you will see God move right away in your life. On many occasions, I have witnessed almost immediate provision when I had decisions to make or needed wisdom and have prayed the wisdom verses out loud.

It might also take time to see the promise that you are praying manifest in your life. Joel Osteen's mother was healed a little at a time over a very long period. Don't get discouraged when you don't see results right away. While you wait, stand firm on God's promise, and be sure you are not moved by your circumstances or by other people's words. Don't allow what you see or feel to change your stance. Continue believing the Word of God. During your wait, you will not only develop a stronger faith, but also a better understanding with the Lord that would otherwise be impossible.

"Therefore the LORD will wait, that He may be gracious to you. And therefore He will be exalted, that He may have mercy on you. For the LORD is a God of justice; Blessed are all those who wait for Him" (Isaiah 30:18, NKJV).

I love the verse in the Bible that says, "Jesus did many other things as well. If every one of them were written down, I suppose that even the whole world would not have room for the books that would be written" (John 21:25, NIV).

As God moves in your life, please write about it. If you keep a journal of what God does in your life, you will be amazed at His provision. God may also use your testimony to encourage others—even your grandchildren or great-grandchildren years down the road.

These words from Revelation 12:11 should motivate us: "And they overcame him by the blood of the Lamb, and by the word of their testimony" (KJV).

If you would like to send me an e-mail of your experiences, I would love to hear from you! E-mail *childlikefaith@juno.com.* I enjoy hearing stories of how God moves in the lives of His people.

I searched for a verse on *BibleGateway.com* one morning, and one of their links led me to *Gospel.com.* As I explored their website, I discovered the following quote, and I absolutely loved it:

> "An elderly Methodist lay preacher named Uncle Am always had assurance his prayer would be answered. A young preacher asked for his secret. He said, 'Young man, learn to plead the promises of God.'"[3]

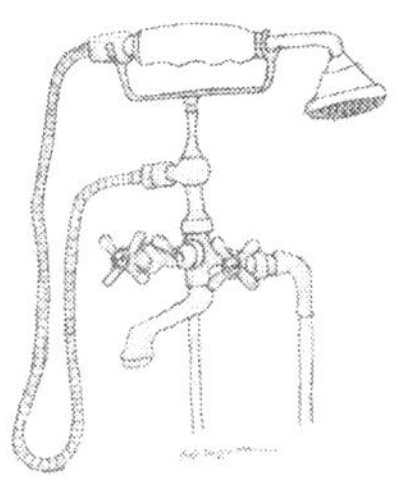

Enjoy the Warm Water

You might be thinking to yourself that spending time with God and developing a relationship with Him sounds great, but your life is busy, and you don't have the time. I have learned that I have more time than I once thought. If you are someone with a very tight schedule, you may have to be a little more creative.

I have found that one of my favorite times with the Lord is in the morning as I clean up and get dressed for the day. Years ago, this time of the morning was my least favorite time of the day. Negative thoughts flooded my mind, and I always began my day with worry. But since I have started using this time to worship and talk to the Lord, it has become one of my favorite times of the day.

I have found that some of my most memorable times with God are in the most unexpected places. One cold winter morning several years ago, I was washing my face. I began to pray and talk to the Lord about some problems that were on my mind. I remember thinking about how great the warm water felt on my face and how it seemed to energize me. I felt God's presence and felt in my spirit that He gave me these thoughts:

> This warm water represents Me and My words. If you will keep your thoughts and focus on Me and My Word and have faith in Me, then you will find peace. Just like the warm water, My presence and My words will soothe and relax you. You will be filled with hope in My promises, and your faith will grow. My grace will warm your heart, and you will feel My love and be comfortable.
>
> If you turn the knob to the cold water, as it hits your skin, you will feel uncomfortable and tense. The cold water represents the world and the enemy's words and ways. That discomfort will lead to irritation, and you will most likely become upset and lose your peace. If you focus on the enemy's negative words and attitudes, then you will experience the same sensations you feel with the cold water. The enemy will fill your spirit with fear and deceit, and he will steal your peace.

Have you ever noticed that a warm shower revives you when you are tired and stressed? Afterward, you feel relaxed and comfortable, as if the water cleansed you from the stress of the world. That is exactly what spending time with God and His Word does for me. His presence in my life cleanses, comforts, and relaxes me. It totally revives me and gives me peace.

The Word says, "I am the Lord your God, who teaches you what is best for you, who directs you in the way you should go. If only you had paid attention to my commands, your peace would have been like a river, your righteousness like the waves of the sea" (Isaiah 48:17–18, NIV).

I do understand that the warm water is tangible and that you can see and feel it hitting your skin. I know a lot of people would say that God is not tangible. It is hard to believe in something that you can't actually see or feel. But I am here to share with you that our God is *real!*

In my experience, the more time I spend getting to know God, the more He allows me to see Him at work in my life. As I spend time focusing on Him and His promises, He allows my eyes to see things the world cannot see. God has promised us in Jeremiah 33:3, "Call to Me and I will answer you and show you great and mighty things, fenced in and hidden, which you do not know (do not distinguish and recognize, have knowledge of and understand)" (AMP).

The Word also tell us, "The entrance and unfolding of [His] Words give light; their unfolding gives understanding (discernment and comprehension) to the simple" (Psalm 119:130, AMP).

Notice that stepping into the shower to be cleansed and refreshed is a choice, and no one forces you to do it. You have to put forth the effort and step into the shower yourself. It is no different with God. He doesn't force Himself on anyone. You have to choose to make God a priority and spend the time with Him that is needed to develop a deep and intimate relationship.

Most of my life, cleanliness has been a bigger priority than time with God. Hardly a day has gone by without me taking a shower or bath, but I have spent many days of my life without spending any time with God. How much more important is having my spirit renewed and cleansed than my physical body?

If most of us approached our daily cleanliness like we do our time with the Lord, it would not be pretty. We would smell bad and be very unpleasant to be around. We would become sick from the bacteria that would grow on our bodies.

I think that sometimes this is what happens with our minds and spirits. Without daily time with the Lord and His Word, our minds become dirty with unforgiveness, anger, and much more. Before long, we become sick from the burdens and worries of this world, and we can eventually become very unpleasant to be around. Without time with God and His Word, the windows of our spirit become dirty, and eventually God's light can no longer be seen through us.

I find it quite interesting that in Ephesians 5:26, there is actually a reference of being cleansed by "the washing of water with the Word" (AMP).

~

Through some of my experiences the last couple of years, I have shared with you how God has taught me the significance of spending quality time with Him and His Word. As I encourage you to spend time with the Lord, I put a tremendous emphasis on incorporating His words into your prayer life. He has taught me that there is power in uniting His holy words with prayer. But at this time, I must bring to your attention that the key to this divine power and to our relationship with God is faith.

"Let us fix our eyes on Jesus, the author and perfecter of our faith, who for the joy set before him endured the cross, scorning its shame, and sat down at the right hand of the throne of God" (Hebrews 12:2, NIV).

In a previous chapter, we studied the first half of the verse from Hebrews 11:6: "And without faith it is impossible to please God." Let's look at the rest of this verse now:

> "Because anyone who comes to Him must believe that He exists and that He rewards those who earnestly seek Him" (NIV).

Let's also look at one last quote by Jim Cymbala from his book, *Fresh Faith:*

> "My life or yours has only as much of God as our faith permits."[1]

There is much more to the act of praying God's Word than merely speaking the words. We must have faith. In Romans 4:13 the Word says, "It was not through the law that Abraham and his offspring received the promise that he would be heir of the world, but through the righteousness that comes by faith" (NIV).

In Hebrews chapter 11, we are reminded of many "who by faith conquered kingdoms, performed acts of righteousness, obtained promises, shut the mouths of lions, quenched the power of fire, escaped the edge of the sword, from weakness were made strong, became mighty in war, put foreign armies to flight" (Hebrews 11:33-34, NASB). Notice verse 33 actually mentions obtaining promises. It is only through faith that we obtain the promises of God. God's power is released by faith.

The condition of the heart also plays a very important role in one's prayer life and relationship with God. God reminds us of this in Isaiah

29:13, "These people come near to me with their mouth and honor me with their lips, but their hearts are far from me" (NIV). We must approach God and speak His Word with the right motives. Simply speaking the Word of God without faith to gain a desired result is not acceptable. In James 4:3, we are told, "When you ask, you do not receive, because you ask with wrong motives, that you may spend what you get on your pleasures" (NIV).

God is sovereign, and He knows our hearts. In fact, we must also approach Him with a pure heart. If our heart is not pure, then even our praises will be unacceptable to Him.[2] What exactly do I mean by this? Sin comes between us and God.

This is better conveyed in Isaiah 59:1-2: "The LORD'S hand is not so short that it cannot save; nor is His ear so dull that it cannot hear. But your iniquities have made a separation between you and your God, and your sins have hidden His face from you so that He does not hear" (NASB).

In 1 John 1:8 we are warned, "If we say that we have no sin, we are deceiving ourselves, and the truth is not in us." Verse 9 goes on to say, "If we confess our sins, He is faithful and righteous to forgive us our sins and to cleanse us from all unrighteousness" (NASB). However, I must add that as we respectfully approach God, aware of our shortcomings and regretfully express our remorse for our sins, we must be willing to change our minds and purpose. We must strive to make a change for the better.

Keep in mind that through Jesus our sins have been nailed to the cross. We must also be willing to accept God's forgiveness and not harbor sin in our hearts.[3] God has taught me that this is a big obstacle in a believer's prayer life—a battle with the enemy, you might say. The enemy does not make it easy for us to grasp this reality.

In 1 John 3:21 we are reminded, "If our hearts do not condemn us, we have confidence before God" (NIV). And in Ephesians 3:12, the Word tells us, "In Him and through faith in Him we may approach God with freedom and confidence" (NIV).

Although as we approach God in prayer, we must also be aware of these words from Daniel 9:18: "We do not make requests of You because we are righteous, but because of Your great mercy" (NIV).

Let me take you back to the image I shared with you earlier of the precious baby girl who caught my attention that memorable Sunday morning. Please realize that the Lord is watching you and gazing into your eyes with admiration. He adores you and thinks that you are wonderful. Never forget that you are precious to Him just like the little baby girl. God is incredible! He loves you just the way you are—no matter what you have done.

For some reason, we always think that we have to be perfect, and think that God gets mad at us if we don't do everything right. The enemy condemns us and makes us feel guilty, which creates an illusion that God loves us less or doesn't care for us at all. We make it hard, but it is really quite simple. God *delights* in you! He longs to be in a relationship with you.

In Matthew 11:28-30 Jesus tells us, "Come to me, all you who are weary and burdened, and I will give you rest. Take my yoke upon you and learn from me, for I am gentle and humble in heart, and you will find rest for your souls. For my yoke is easy and my burden is light" (NIV).

God is eagerly waiting to spend time with you. "The LORD your God in your midst, The Mighty One, will save; He will rejoice over you with gladness, He will quiet you with His love, He will rejoice over you with singing" (Zephaniah 3:17, NKJV).

If you don't have a relationship with Him or have fallen away from Him, *please* spend some time with Him and talk to Him. He loves you so much that He allowed His only Son to be beaten and crucified on a cross to save *you*. "God so loved the world that he gave his one and only

Son, that whoever believes in him shall not perish but have eternal life" (John 3:16, NIV).

God's love is inconceivable! For me, the experience of comprehending the overwhelming love of Christ through this sweet little girl those brief moments in time was a gift from God. I hope you will accept the same gift today.

This quote really sums it up for me. It is a quote by Charles Spurgeon from *Streams in the Desert:*

> "O people of God, be great believers! Little faith will bring your souls to heaven, but great faith will bring heaven to your souls."[4]

Beware of the Camel

I believe one of the biggest misconceptions about God today is the issue of control. We do not want to give up control of our lives. From the moment Robert received his diagnosis, I felt that all control of my life had been stripped away from us—and in reality, it had. The enemy used this reality to try to get me to be angry at God and give up on my relationship with Him. It wasn't until later that I began to better understand that this was not only a misconception, but that I had actually been given a gift from God.

I have always been one of those people who needed control of my life. You might even go as far as to say that I was a control freak. But over the last few years, God has taught me that the life which I led was far from the life that He had planned for me. The enemy had convinced me that I was where I needed to be in my relationship with God, and I was very comfortable.

Years ago, when my daughter was very young, my husband took a business trip out of state. My daughter and I decided that we would tag along with him on the trip and do some sightseeing. One afternoon, we decided to visit a wild animal park. I had purchased a new car just months before driving through this Animal Park.

As we drove down the path at the park and enjoyed all the different animals, we were forced to come to an abrupt stop. Sitting in the road in front of us was a large camel. I began to blow my horn and wait for the camel to move. After several minutes, I realized that he had no intention of moving any time soon. I took the only obvious choice and retreated. After recognizing that there were no other cars behind me, I put my car into reverse and began to back up until we returned to the office of the park. We quickly ran into the building and were immediately met by one of the employees of the park. The employee had an annoyingly playful grin on her face and approached us as if she had been expecting our return. I told her about the issue we had with the camel, and she began to laugh. As she chuckled, she explained that the camel enjoyed harassing the visitors, and if I would just keep driving forward with momentum toward him, he would eventually move. She continued to explain that this habit of bothering the visitors seemed to be his favorite pastime.

Well, to say the least, I was not at all amused by her humor, and I was becoming more and more frustrated by the minute. Hiding my frustration, I kindly thanked her for the information, and my daughter and I went on our way to continue our adventure.

As we once again approached the camel sitting stubbornly in the middle of the road, I slowly drove closer. Just as I had been instructed, I continued to roll towards him. Again, the camel didn't budge. I could have sworn that I saw the old camel smile as he looked at me mischievously.

It was at this time, as I sat in my shiny new car, that I had a decision to make. Did I have the courage to do what I had been instructed, even when it didn't make sense to me? At this particular point in time, I was already much closer to the old camel than I would have ever imagined possible. After determining this path was the only way out of the park, I decided that I would just trust what the woman had told me and go for it. I put my car in reverse and backed up a few feet, thinking I might intimidate him a little. I then said a prayer, shifted to drive, and moved forward with some speed—just as I had been instructed. My car was maybe an inch from the camel before he jumped up and moved out of the road.

So what does this story have to do with God? It is all about faith! It took an act of faith to drive towards the camel without stopping. But when I did as I was instructed—even when it didn't make any sense to me logically—the camel moved, just as I had been told.

Entering into a deeper relationship with God will require faith. When you begin to do things God's way, you will be required to step out on faith. He will ask you to live inside certain boundaries. Although we might not always understand the reasons behind them, within these boundaries, God will lead and guide you—but most importantly, He will protect and provide for you.

Let me better explain by sharing one of my personal experiences with tithing. Tithing is a great way to put your faith into action.

When Robert was diagnosed with aplastic anemia, we realized it could easily bankrupt us. We are paid on a monthly basis, and when I sat down a few days after his diagnosis to write our tithe check to the church, all I could hear in my head was, "Don't do it! You will need this money!" But I knew those negative thoughts were not coming from God and were just lies. I also knew that God was faithful, so I didn't think twice when writing the check.

Robert was unable to work for two months, but we were completely taken care of financially by God. He had no short term disability program at his place of employment, but he received his paycheck both months. We met our out-of-pocket maximum with our health insurance which was $4,000.00 within a few days. There were also charges which weren't covered under our policy and charges the insurance wouldn't pay. We quickly acquired some very large medical bills.

We didn't go around talking about the medical bills that were adding up. I knew that somehow God would help us if we just continued to tithe. Before long, an amazing thing began to happen. People began to randomly give us money. We received checks and cash from family, friends, church members, and coworkers. We were receiving money from people we didn't even know. We even came home one day to find over a hundred dollars in cash which someone had stuck in our front door. After all the gifts and medical expenses were totaled, we discovered that we had received enough to pay off our medical bills—almost to the penny. God is incredible!

"The LORD is faithful to all His promises and loving toward all He has made" (Psalm 145:13, NIV).

To say the least, I now have a much stronger understanding on the subject of tithing. I was raised by a family of believers. My parents tithed, and I had been taught all about giving from a very young age. But when I started out on my own, I was convinced I couldn't afford to give—although deep in my heart, I knew that I was missing something.

After Robert and I were married (even with two incomes), I was convinced that we couldn't afford to faithfully tithe. Again, my husband's income was based on commissions, so when things were good, we tithed—but when business was slow, we stopped. I knew I wasn't doing things God's way. I always seemed to be shocked when we could never get ahead; I still knew deep in my heart that I was missing something.

One Sunday morning at our church, a couple gave their testimony about tithing. I was touched by their story, and I never forgot it. Although it was a couple of years until Robert and I finally had the courage to step out and faithfully tithe our gross income, God used the couples' testimony to give us the strength we needed to be obedient. We felt confident that if God would so boldly provide for the couple at our church, then He would certainly provide for us. "I now realize how true it is that God does not show favoritism" (Acts 10:34, NIV).

Before Robert and I began to faithfully and joyfully tithe, we just didn't get it. We *were* missing something. Tithing isn't about money, really. It isn't logical to us, and I certainly still don't understand God's ways, but one of the most important things to know about tithing is that it isn't about the money. God doesn't *need* our money! He is God! He is the Creator of the universe and everything in it! It is about a relationship with a supernatural God. It is that simple. Do we believe that God is real, and do we trust Him?

When you are trying to do things God's way and you find yourself at a crossroad, your actions are a sign to God of what you believe. The enemy will try anything and everything to attempt to convince you and me that we just can't do it. Those negative thoughts which run through our minds will try to convince us that we just can't do things God's way and survive—we will not make it financially. They will try to convince us that it isn't wise to give money away when you can clearly see that there isn't enough money to get through the week or month. We will be tempted to believe that it isn't good business to give 10 percent of your income away while you have debt.

Again, I will remind you that the enemy knows God is real. He knows when you take a step out and start faithfully giving, you will then be in the position to better see God work in your life! He knows that those steps of faith will open the door for God to pour out his blessings and move in your life.

God loves you, and He is waiting for you to step out and make the first move. Money can buy you many things on this earth that will make you happy momentarily—and sometimes even long-term—but you will never find the peace and happiness that comes from God alone anywhere on this earth.

"The world and its desires pass away, but whoever does the will of God lives forever" (1 John 2:17, NIV).

Let me once again remind you of this promise from God. Jeremiah 29:11 says, "'For I know the plans I have for you,' declares the LORD, 'plans to prosper you and not to harm you, plans to give you hope and a future'" (NIV).

This is a promise which you can count on—but you do have to do things God's way. You won't ever experience God's best if you don't step out and prove to Him that you really do believe—even when it doesn't make sense to you.

God actually challenges us to tithe in Malachi 3:10: "'Bring the whole tithe into the storehouse, that there may be food in my house. Test me in this,' says the LORD Almighty, 'and see if I will not throw open the floodgates of heaven and pour out so much blessing that you will not have room enough for it'" (NIV).

~

The next thoughts I want to share with you will require you to use your imagination. Just for a few moments, imagine that you are driving down a very narrow country road. This road represents your life. It may represent a life with an established relationship with God, or it might represent a life that is unfamiliar with God.

As you travel down this road, you approach a closed gate blocking the road. This gate contains an old-fashioned automatic opener. If a driver stops before approaching the gate, it will not open. But if the driver drives straight toward it, the weight of the car will compress the springs under the road, and the gate will open.

Imagine that this gate represents the only entrance to a better life—a life of freedom and peace—and the only thing that is keeping you from entering this life is the gate. The gate is closed.

Obviously, if you didn't understand and hadn't been informed about this gate when you approached it, you would stop. But if you had knowledge and understanding of the opener, you most likely would approach the gate without stopping. To continue driving towards a closed gate without stopping isn't logical unless you have been instructed otherwise.

Even if you have been instructed and understand the gate's mechanics, your decision to continue driving toward the closed gate will require some faith. As you approach the gate, what you do next will depend on what you believe.

It is at this time that the enemy will begin to work overtime trying to stop you. The enemy doesn't want you to know that through this gate is a life of freedom. He is a lot like the old camel sitting in the road at the Animal Park—the major difference being that the camel could clearly be seen. The enemy will remind you that driving through this gate will require giving up control of your life and try to convince you the gate represents only boundaries. He doesn't want you to know that by doing things God's way, you will actually receive an amazing gift. He will do anything possible to make it look very undesirable to you. But remember the butterfly—things are not always as they seem. If he doesn't succeed with this strategy, then he might also use doubt and fear to manipulate you into believing that stopping—which requires no risk—will be much more comfortable and safe.

For years, I sat at this gate. I was well versed in my relationship with God and completely understood the mechanics of the believer's life. But as I approached the gate, I wasn't prepared for the enemy. I became fearful and stopped short of the life that God had planned for me. The enemy even convinced me that I was comfortable and safe sitting at the gate.

So it all comes down to this—what do you believe? No matter where you are in your faith—whether you are just approaching or have already stopped and are sitting at the gate—what will you do? Will you ignore the enemy? Will you put your childlike faith into action, find freedom, and experience the wonderful life which Jesus died for you to have?

Don't stop at the gate!

> "Open for me the gates of righteousness; I will enter and give thanks to the LORD. This is the gate of the LORD through which the righteous may enter. I will give you thanks, for you answered me; you have become my salvation" (Psalm 118:19–21, NIV).

Honey From the Rock

Life is a journey, and every person travels down a different path and fights different battles. Just as God holds the hands of my family members down the path of aplastic anemia, He will guide you through even the toughest of circumstances by His amazing grace. The challenge is to not get angry with God, to complain, or fight Him because you don't want to give in to His plans. Embrace and trust Him more than ever at these times, and praise Him—especially when things are not going your way.

As you wait for God to get you through to the other side of the unpleasant experience, be sure to always remember to keep your spiritual eyes open. Stay on the lookout for opportunities to share your faith with others. Doing this will place you in a position to learn more about God. Choose to look at every threatening circumstance as an opportunity to spread your wings of faith and fly higher with Him.

If you don't see any evidence of God moving in your circumstances during this waiting period, please do not become discouraged. God tells us in Daniel 10:12, "Since the first day that you set your mind to gain understanding and to humble yourself before your God, your words were heard, and I have come in response to them" (NIV). Please don't give up on Him. It is at these times that we are offered the opportunity to prove to God what we really believe. Allow your actions to prove to Him that you really do trust Him.

Depend on Him as a child looks to a parent, and hold tightly to Him. He is your Father, and He loves you! He is all that you need. Don't focus on your circumstances and your feelings, but focus on Him and feed on His promises. Spend time praising Him, being obedient, and loving others while trusting Him completely to get you through any circumstance. In return, He will work everything out for good—just as He has promised. It is through these times that you will learn just how faithful and alive God really is.

> "For I will surely deliver you; and you shall not fall by the sword, but your life shall be as a prize to you, because you have put your trust in Me, says the Lord. (Jeremiah 39:18, NKJV).

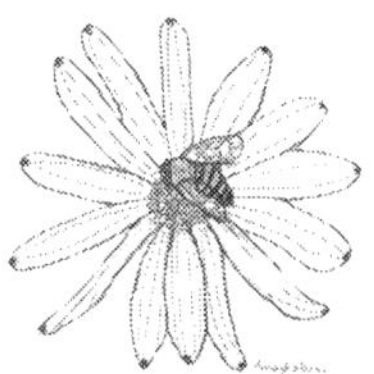

> "My son, eat honey, because it is good, and the drippings of the honeycomb are sweet to your taste. So shall you know skillful and godly Wisdom to be thus to your life; if you find it, then shall there be a future and a reward, and your hope and expectation shall not be cut off" (Proverbs 24:13–14, AMP).

One night, several years before I began writing, I had a dream about this book. I could actually see the book, and I held it in my hands. It was an amazing experience, and when I was awakened from my dream, I had only one thing on my mind. All I could think about were honey bees. As strange as it sounds, this truly is what was on my mind. As I questioned my thoughts and spent some time with the Lord, I began to have a better understanding of what it all meant. The following is an excerpt from my journal that day:

> As a child of God, a believer's spiritual life is similar to that of a honey bee. As God directs us down each path, we learn and draw wisdom from every experience—just

as the honey bee flies from bloom to bloom, collecting pollen and nectar. God allows us to experience different circumstances to teach us and help us to grow. As the honeybee gathers the nectar, it takes the pollen grains from one flower to another, which is familiar to all as cross-pollination. As we each walk down the paths that God has planned for us, we fellowship with others and are offered opportunities to share our faith and plant seeds—just like the bee.

The pollen and nectar are carried back to the hive, and there the bees process and produce a delicious honey that is collected by humans to be eaten and enjoyed. As we believers travel down these paths and as we grow and learn, we experience God and are drawn closer to Him. We take the wisdom which we have gained and develop a better understanding of God and become more familiar with His character.

With this knowledge, we not only strive to become more like Him, but hopefully at the end of each path, we allow God to transform us into wiser and stronger believers—each experiencing God in our own individual ways and each with our own unique stories. We then share the love of God and our experiences and lessons learned or testimonies with others. These testimonies are just like the honey—sweet and only produced by God.

~

"In a desert land he found him, in a barren and howling waste. He shielded him and cared for him; he guarded him as the apple of his eye, like an eagle that stirs up its nest and hovers over its young, that spreads its wings to catch them and carries them on its pinions. The LORD alone led him; no foreign god was with him.

> He made him ride on the heights of the land and fed him with the fruit of the fields. He nourished him with honey from the rock, and with oil from the flinty crag" (Deuteronomy 32:10–13, NIV).

~

God is our rock! We hope you have been nourished by the honey produced from the Rock in our desert.

> "So do not fear, for I am with you; do not be dismayed, for I am your God. I will strengthen you and help you; I will uphold you with my righteous right hand.
>
> For I am the LORD your God who takes hold of your right hand and says to you, do not fear; I will help you.
>
> The poor and needy search for water, but there is none; their tongues are parched with thirst. But I the LORD will answer them; I, the God of Israel, will not forsake them. I will make rivers flow on barren heights, and springs within the valleys. I will turn the desert into pools of water, and the parched ground into springs. I will put in the desert the cedar and the acacia, the myrtle and the olive. I will set pines in the wasteland, the fir and the cypress together, so that people may see and know, may consider and understand, that the hand of the LORD has done this, that the Holy One of Israel has created it" (Isaiah 41:10, 13, 17–20, NIV).

Our Deliverer

As I stumbled to the bathroom early one morning, I suddenly felt that the Lord wanted my attention. I paused for a couple of moments and knelt down to worship and thank God for His presence in my life. After turning my focus completely on Him, I heard the following statement in my head: *This will be a day like no other!*

As I showered and dressed, I was reminded of a few verses that I felt appropriate to pray on this particular morning. I prayed the following verses aloud as I prepared for my day:

> "Who am I, O Sovereign LORD, and what is my family, that you have brought me this far? And as if this were not enough in your sight, O Sovereign LORD, you have also spoken about the future of the house of your servant. Is this your usual way of dealing with man, O Sovereign LORD? For you know your servant, O Sovereign LORD. For the sake of your word and according to your will, you have done this great thing and made it known to your servant. And now, LORD God, keep forever the promise you have made concerning your servant and his house. Do as you promised, so that your name will be great forever" (2 Samuel 7:18–21, 25–26, NIV).

I then began to think about my life, and I took a few moments to reflect back over the last couple of years. Memories flooded my mind as I thought back on how far Robert and I had come. The journey has been very difficult, but through the precious grace and presence of our Lord, it has been an amazing one. As we have turned to God and held on to Him through this journey, He has blessed us in countless ways. As I thought about the level of intimacy I experienced with the Lord, I began to think of how our lives will look and feel when God delivers Robert from the complications of this disease. Suddenly, I became very fearful. Although I immediately recognized that this fear was certainly not coming from God, I didn't completely understand. Shouldn't these thoughts bring me joy and some type of relief?

As my mind raced to search for answers, I suddenly understood. For over two years now, I have believed and waited for God to deliver us from this disease. Now that the day was upon us, I realized that *I had already been delivered!*

I have been praying and believing the promises of God to deliver me *out* of my circumstances, but through these experiences and times of waiting on God, I suddenly realized that He has delivered me *in* my circumstances.

As I continued to search my thoughts, I came to the realization that although I certainly wanted Robert delivered from this disease, I feared losing the connection and intimacy I had with the Father. Through the challenges of aplastic anemia, I entered into the most wonderful relationship with the Lord, and it is one I never even knew existed. I was set free through these circumstances, and it has certainly been obvious that my Father knew what was best for me.

"The LORD will guide you always; he will satisfy your needs in a sun-scorched land and will strengthen your frame. You will be like a well-watered garden, like a spring whose waters never fail" (Isaiah 58:11, NIV).

A couple hours after this encounter, Robert and I eagerly arrived at the doctor's office for our six-week checkup. The day was exactly two years and three months from the day of Robert's diagnosis. Our hearts were once again filled with anticipation, as we patiently waited for the results of Robert's blood work. As I waited, I couldn't help but remember the statement that rang in my head earlier in the morning: *This will be a day like no other!*

After being called back to the examining room, the anticipation grew stronger as each minute passed. We once again found ourselves being taught by the Lord the act of patience. Our expectations grew as we waited for the results.

Today was the day! Robert's platelet count was in the normal range for the first time! His white and red blood cells had also risen, and were extremely close to the normal range. Many aplastic anemia patients never witness their platelets ever rising to the normal range. The doctor lowered the dosage of the steroids by half and said that if things continued to go well, he would start weaning Robert off the cyclosporine on our next visit.

My mind couldn't help but wander back to thoughts of our sling and stone and the verses from 1 Samuel 17:45–47. These are the words of David as he prepared for battle with Goliath: "You come against me with sword and spear and javelin, but I come against you in the name of the LORD Almighty, the God of the armies of Israel, whom you have defied. This day the LORD will hand you over to me, and I'll strike you down and cut off your head. Today I will give the carcasses of the Philistine army to the birds of the air and the beasts of the earth, and the whole world will know that there is a God in Israel. All those gathered here will know that it is not by sword or spear that the LORD saves; for the battle is the LORD's, and he will give all of you into our hands" (NIV).

The wonderful sling and stone symbolize our gift of God's promises and our ammunition from the Father to help us fight the battles of our lives. Our God is so great!

As we drove back home, within just a couple of minutes, a song started playing on the radio. It was "My Deliverer." I knew that this wasn't just a coincidence, and this song was playing at this particular time for a reason. God *is* our Deliverer! He is Jehovah Rapha—the God who heals!

"The LORD is my rock and my fortress and my deliverer; My God, my strength, in whom I will trust; My shield and the horn of my salvation, my stronghold" (Psalm 18:2, NKJV).

As we put our faith into action by speaking and praying God's promises aloud, God *is* faithful to deliver us! Just like David, He equipped my family with everything we needed to save us from our giant, aplastic anemia.

~

> "O Sovereign LORD, my strong deliverer, who shields my head in the day of battle" (Psalm 140:7, NIV).

~

God provided us with an amazing, godly doctor and nurse practitioner, a wonderful staff of nurses, and a great hospital to administer Robert's treatment. He provided amazing friends and family who ministered to us every step of the way. I could go on forever, bragging about all the wonderful things God has done in our lives. He has healed Robert's bone marrow! He also healed me from the wrong mindset and bondage which was holding me back from His best for my life. God alone is to be praised!

You might think that God didn't need us to speak those verses to heal us—and you would be right. Just the act of speaking His Word did not heal us. It is God alone who heals. However, keep in mind that faith pleases God, and speaking and praying God's promises out loud grows our faith. It is also an act of faith; therefore, it pleases Him.

Let's look at one of the many accounts of God's healing in Exodus 15:22–26:

> "Then Moses led Israel from the Red Sea and they went into the Desert of Shur. For three days they traveled in the desert without finding water. When they came to Marah, they could not drink its water because it was bitter. (That is why the place is called Marah.) So the people grumbled against Moses, saying, 'What are we to drink?' Then Moses cried out to the LORD, and the LORD showed him a piece of wood. He threw it into the water, and the water became sweet. There the LORD made a decree and a law for them, and there he tested them. He said, 'If you listen carefully to the voice of the LORD your God and do what is right in his

> eyes, if you pay attention to his commands and keep all his decrees, I will not bring on you any of the diseases I brought on the Egyptians, for I am the LORD, who heals you'" (NIV).

In these verses, the Israelites were dying of thirst. After three days, they finally came upon water—but they couldn't drink it, because the water was bitter. God delivered them in their bad circumstances by healing the waters of Marah and providing drinkable water for them.

Do you believe the actions of Moses picking up the piece of wood and throwing it into the water proved his faith in the Almighty Deliverer?

"Therefore let everyone who is godly pray to you while you may be found; surely when the mighty waters rise, they will not reach him. You are my hiding place; you will protect me from trouble and surround me with songs of deliverance" (Psalm 32:6–7, NIV).

One glorious day, two years, four months, and twenty-one days after Robert's diagnosis of aplastic anemia, he received a phone call delivering his long and anxiously awaited evidence. The doctor and nurse practitioner had just reviewed Robert's most recent bone marrow biopsy results. His nurse practitioner and very dear friend proclaimed, "Robert, you are in remission! Your bone marrow is normal!"

God is our Deliverer!

In Exodus 3:14-15 God instructs Moses: "Thus you shall say to the sons of Israel, 'I AM has sent me to you.' God, furthermore, said to Moses, "Thus you shall say to the sons of Israel, 'The LORD, the God of your fathers, the God of Abraham, the God of Isaac, and the God of Jacob, has sent me to you.' This is My name forever, and this is My memorial-name to all generations" (NASB).

The great "I AM" will deliver you. He cares for you. He is "indeed concerned about you and what has been done to you" (Exodus 3:16, NASB). He "will bring you up out of the affliction" (Exodus 3:17, NASB). He will deliver you from the bondages of this day. Do you feel you are a slave to fear, worry or a destructive bad habit or addiction? Do you suffer from the complications of an illness, disease or physical disability? In Psalm 50:15 the Lord says, "Call upon Me in the day of trouble; I will deliver you and you shall glorify Me" (NKJV).

"The sons of Israel sighed because of the bondage, and they cried out; and *their cry for help because of their bondage rose up to God.* So *God heard their groaning*; and God remembered His covenant with Abraham, Isaac, and Jacob. God saw the sons of Israel, and *God took notice of them*" (Exodus 2:23-25, NASB).

God spoke the following words to Moses concerning the Israelites many years ago, but they are still for us today: "The LORD said, '*I have surely seen the affliction of My people* who are in Egypt, *and have given heed to their cry* because of their taskmasters, for *I am aware of their sufferings.* So *I have come down to deliver them* from the power of the Egyptians, *and to bring them up from that land to a good and spacious land, to a land flowing with milk and honey*'" (Exodus 3:7-8, NASB).

"Jesus Christ is the same yesterday and today and forever" (Hebrews 13:8, NASB).

Let me once again remind you that if God doesn't move in your life in a way that you might expect or desire, please be patient and trust Him with childlike faith. Remember that He is your Father, and He knows what is best for you. You can rest assured that if He doesn't deliver you *out* of your bad circumstances, then He *will* surely deliver you *in* them! Either way, He is faithful! In your troubles, God will heal your bitter waters and make them drinkable and sweet.[1]

> "To him who is able to keep you from falling and to present you before his glorious presence without fault and with great joy—to the only God our Savior be glory, majesty, power and authority, through Jesus Christ our Lord, before all ages, now and forevermore! Amen" (Jude 1:24–25, NIV).

Sing a New Song

One Sunday morning, as I was spending some time with God and preparing to start my day, the following words randomly crossed my mind: *Every knee shall bow.* I recognized that these words were from a verse in the Bible. This definitely got my attention, so I immediately looked up the verse.

The verse is from Philippians 2:5–10: "Your attitude should be the same as that of Christ Jesus: Who, being in very nature God, did not consider equality with God something to be grasped, but made himself nothing, taking the very nature of a servant, being made in human likeness. And being found in appearance as a man, he humbled himself and became obedient to death—even death on a cross! Therefore God exalted him to the highest place and gave him the name that is above every name, that at the name of Jesus every knee should bow, in heaven and on earth and under the earth" (NIV).

As I studied these verses, God began to reveal to me that there was more to speaking and praying God's Word than I realized. It became very apparent that there was much more to understand.

Philippians 2:10 says that God wants every knee to bow to Him. What exactly does it mean to bow your knee to someone? As I began to think about what this actually meant, I realized that bowing is an action of faith. I came to the realization that the act of bowing also takes a certain amount of humility. It is definitely humbling to bow before the Lord and acknowledge Him. I also came to the conclusion that bowing is an act of surrendering one's self—a type of declaration, you might say. This action declares that God is sovereign.

As I searched for more verses on humility, I ran across 1 Peter 5:5–6: "God opposes the proud but gives grace to the humble. Humble yourselves, therefore, under God's mighty hand, that he may lift you up in due time" (NIV). These verses make it very clear that God's desire is for His children to humble themselves before Him.

So what does this have to do with praying God's Word?

Earlier we established that praying God's Word is actually an action of faith. It is also an act of humility. As we replace our words with God's during our time in prayer, we are humbling ourselves before Him acknowledging that His thoughts are higher than our thoughts. As we align our lives with His will through His Word, we are actually surrendering ourselves to Him. We are acknowledging that He is sovereign.

As I continued to study, verse 11 really got my attention. Philippians 2:11 says, "and every tongue confess that Jesus Christ is Lord, to the glory of God the Father" (NIV). This is where the verse gets very interesting. When I see the word *confess,* I usually think it means a confession of sin. Let's look at the other meanings of this word from *Dictionary.com:* "to acknowledge one's belief or faith in; declare adherence to, or to own or admit as true."[1]

Do you see where I am going with this?

In Hebrews 13:15, the Word also says, "Through Jesus, therefore, let us continually offer to God a *sacrifice of praise*—the fruit of lips that openly profess his name" (NIV). God wants us to confess or acknowledge our belief and faith in Him as a type of praise and worship.

This is where we get into the difference between actually praying God's Word out loud and praying it silently. As we pray and choose to speak God's Word in place of our own words, we are confessing that God exists and He is sovereign. This type of confession acknowledges our belief and faith in Him. We are making His promises our own and admitting that His Word is true. This action of faith is not only an act of obedience (as we see in Hebrews 13:15), but also an act of offering and an actual *sacrifice of praise.* This is truly a type of worship. With the right motives, this action takes us to a higher degree or level of worship with God.

When you think about it, this action is similar to raising our hands as we worship God. When done with the right motives, this action of faith also places us into a higher degree of worship.

Please notice that these actions of faith require most of us to step out of our comfort zones. I used to feel very uncomfortable raising my hands to worship God—especially in public. It was out of my comfort zone. But over time, as my relationship with God has grown and I better understand the amazing God I serve, this action of faith has become a very important part of my worship. God is worthy of our praise!

When God began to teach me the importance of speaking His Word out loud through prayer, I also felt quite awkward at first, even though I was in my home and I prayed them in my personal time with the Lord. This act of faith also required me to step out of my comfort zone a bit. But now, I can't imagine my personal time with God without His Word being a part of it. God's Word has become such a part of my life that praying it aloud seems natural, and I enjoy the special connection with the Lord.

Most every act of faith and obedience to God requires us to step out of our comfort zones—at least in the beginning. Recently, while talking to a friend of mine on this subject, I came to a very interesting realization. She brought to my attention that speaking God's Word out loud is only out of our comfort zones in certain settings. Most of us are very comfortable reading His Word out loud in our church or in a Bible study. But isn't it interesting that in our everyday lives, this action seems to push most of us out of our comfort levels?

I am in no way insinuating that reading and praying God's Word in this manner is the only effective type of prayer and worship. I spend plenty of time sharing what is on my heart with the Lord and reading His Word silently. Spending time with God, worshiping Him, and spending time in His Word is what is most important. However, as I have incorporated God's Word into my prayers, I have experienced God in a more powerful way.

This is the bottom line: God is always willing and able to act mightily in our lives, but He waits on us to act on our faith. Our actions of faith and obedience are very pertinent to our relationship with Him. The Bible tells us in James 2:26, "For as the body without the spirit is dead, so faith without works is dead also" (NKJV).

Will we humbly take those steps or actions of faith that prove to God that we want and need more of Him? Will we live our lives in such a way as to show God that He is a priority? Will we place God and His Word first in our lives?

In Deuteronomy 6:6–9, God tells us, "These words which I am commanding you this day shall be [first] in your [own] minds and hearts; [then] You shall whet and sharpen them so as to make them penetrate, and teach and impress them diligently upon the [minds and] hearts of your children, and shall talk of them when you sit in your house and when you walk by the way, and when you lie down and when you rise up. And you shall bind them as a sign upon your hand, and they shall be as frontlets (forehead bands) between your eyes. And you shall write them upon the doorposts of your house and on your gates" (AMP).

Earlier we learned through scripture that faith pleases God, and our faith grows by hearing the Word. We now learn from these verses that God wants us to put His Word front and center in our minds and hearts. These verses make it very clear this is exactly what God wants for His people. Incorporating God's Word into our prayer lives is certainly a great way to do this.

Have you ever noticed that as you read quietly to yourself, your mind has a tendency to stray to other things? Do you sometimes completely lose your concentration? On the other hand, have you noticed that if you speak the words as you read them, it is much easier to control your train of thought? As we pray, if we speak God's Word in place of our own, the Word cannot be any closer to our minds. This type of meditation truly places God's Word first in our minds and hearts.

I really love David's prayer in Psalm 19:14: "May the words of my mouth and the meditation of my heart be pleasing in your sight, O LORD, my Rock and my Redeemer" (NIV). What better way to please God than for His words to be coming out of our mouths?

~

A little over a year ago, my daughter was getting ready to graduate from high school, and I felt the pain that most parents feel as they prepare for their children to begin college. As I tried to accept the fact that my little girl was all grown up, I struggled with the flood of emotions I experienced. After all, the last nineteen years of my life had been mainly focused on raising her, since she was my only child. This was going to be a big adjustment for me.

I began to pray and ask God exactly what He had in store for me at this point in my life. One morning, several days after I began this prayer, I was spending some time with Him as I dressed for the day. The following statement ran across my mind: *You will sing a new song.* I immediately knew that this was from God, but I didn't have a clue what it meant. However, I did feel confident that He would help me understand when He was ready in His perfect timing. This statement continued to ring in my head quite often for months after this experience.

More than a year later, I was still very curious as to what it meant for me to "sing a new song." I can carry a tune—but that's not saying much. I am certainly not gifted in this area. I knew that this could have nothing to do with my actual singing ability (or the lack thereof).

A few weeks after Robert received the news that he was in remission, he and I returned to see the doctor and nurse practitioner to discuss his test results and our plan of action to wean him off his medications. That evening, as I tried to settle down from the exciting day we had experienced, I spent some time silently thanking and praising God for what He had done. I suddenly felt the Lord's presence very strongly, and I felt led to spend some time with Him in His Word. I picked up my Bible and randomly opened it and began to read the verses on the page. Amazingly enough, these were the words I read from Psalm 40:1–5:

> "I waited patiently for the LORD; he turned to me and heard my cry. He lifted me out of the slimy pit, out of the mud and mire; he set my feet on a rock and gave me a firm place to stand. *He put a new song in my mouth, a hymn of praise to our God.* Many will see and fear and

> put their trust in the LORD. Blessed is the man who makes the LORD his trust, who does not look to the proud, to those who turn aside to false gods. Many, O LORD my God, are the wonders you have done. The things you planned for us no one can recount to you; were I to speak and tell of them, they would be too many to declare" (NIV).

Tears streamed down my face as I read these amazing words. This was my answer! I was overwhelmed by God's goodness. "The Lord is my Strength and Song" (Psalm 118:14, AMP), and His words are my hymn of praise.

"Sing to the LORD a new song, for he has done marvelous things" (Psalm 98:1, NIV).

Interestingly enough, I searched, and I couldn't find this exact phrase anywhere else in the Bible.

I encourage you to put a new song in your mouth; a hymn of praise to your God. Acknowledge your belief in Him, and put your childlike faith into action. Spend time with God in prayer, humbly confessing His Word out of your mouth as your sacrifice of praise. *Sing a new song!*

"Sing to the LORD a new song; sing to the LORD, all the earth" (Psalm 96:1, NIV).

Conclusion

I never want to forget the day in the hospital when I waited for my husband's test results. Robert and I received much more than a diagnosis that day. This was the day we began an amazing journey with God—a journey that would allow us the privilege of experiencing His healing hand, and one that would set me free (John 8:32).

God has graciously allowed this opportunity and supplied the words for me to share some of our testimony with you. As for the ability to adequately describe the presence of the Holy Spirit in our lives these past several years, I lack that ability. Those words do not exist. With respect to that inability, I shall end with this simple statement: we have truly witnessed the glory of God! (John 11:40)

We are thankful.

"Declare His glory among the nations, His marvelous deeds among all peoples" (1 Chronicles 16:24, NIV).

"Be joyful in hope, patient in affliction, faithful in prayer" (Romans 12:12, NIV).

Afterword

I find myself living in a continual state of awe at God's creation as the seasons change each year. God amazes me every year as He orchestrates each unique season to carry out nature's agenda. Just as it is with nature, every season in our lives is designed to carry out our Creator's perfect plan and "purpose" (Ecclesiastes 3:1, AMP).

This fall, I once again found myself admiring my favorite wild cherry tree. Imagine my surprise when the leaves of this tree became the most brilliant in our entire yard. I couldn't help but feel that God himself had painted each leaf especially for me.

As I thought back to that memorable summer afternoon with the Lord while watering the flowers in my back yard, it was very evident to me that there were additional lessons to be learned from this tree.

Before Robert was diagnosed with aplastic anemia, I was a so-called happy believer, and I was very comfortable in my relationship with the Lord. I read a devotion every morning, which always contained a few verses of God's Word. I attended church regularly on Sundays, where I heard the Word of God. I even attended a small group from my church and participated in a Bible study. However, I am now convinced that my spirit was thirsty.

As God's living Word flooded my life and began to penetrate my heart as I consumed it, my spirit began to receive the water it so desperately needed. Jesus began to grow my faith and spirit stronger as His "living water" (John 4:10) revived and healed me. Jesus speaks of this "living water" in John 4:14: "Whoever drinks of the water that I shall give him will never thirst. But the water that I shall give him will become in him a fountain of water springing up into everlasting life" (NKJV).

I have since encountered another interesting experience with the Lord as I sat down to eat my lunch one day during the editing of this book. I was very hungry, and after heating my food, I sat down to enjoy it. After taking a couple of bites, I became very aware of the presence of God. In a small, quiet voice in my head, I heard God ask me to stop eating and spend some time with Him. I was very hesitant at first, because this was so unexpected. After all, could I not spend time with Him after I finished my lunch? As pathetic as it sounds, this is exactly what went through my mind. Not eating my lunch seemed a tiny bit radical to me. Followers of Jesus are risking their lives all over the world, yet this seemed radical to me.

Looking back on this, I find it funny that when God asks me to do something which sounds reasonable, I am eager to obey. But if He asks me to do something out of the ordinary requiring me to give up something, I automatically brand it "radical" and question whether I have actually heard from God.

With this being said, I immediately began to question myself, wondering if this was truly God. And if it was God, why would He want me to stop eating to spend time with Him? Couldn't I just worship Him while I ate? It just didn't make sense to me. Unbelievably enough, I sat for a minute, debating on what to do.

After I spent a short time on my knees worshiping God, I then began to ask Him a few questions. "God, why would you ask me to stop eating? My food was hot, and I was hungry." I was obviously still trying to change His mind. His only response to me was that I would find my nourishment from Him.

If I could get past the embarrassment and shame of my actions, I would actually be quite amused by them as I look back on this experience. I talked back to my Father—just like my child occasionally talks back to me when she doesn't like what I have asked her to do.

God began to bring to my mind all His children around the world who are hungry and have nothing to eat. I suddenly became very aware that the hunger I was experiencing had already been satisfied once that day with breakfast. I began to think of how much stronger my appetite would have been if I hadn't had anything else to eat that day—or maybe even the day before. I was very humbled and no longer questioned God at this point. I began to relax and come to my senses. I didn't need this hamburger as much as I needed Him. What in the world had I been thinking?

I became overwhelmed by the goodness of God, and I spent some time praising and thanking Him for His provision and praying for those who were hungry.

God then shared with me that in every believer's spirit, He has placed an appetite that can only be satisfied by Him and His Word. This is more important than any earthly nourishment. He reminded me that I need to always be grateful and remember His provision. He also reminded me that He was a "jealous God" (Exodus 20:5), and without Him, I can do nothing.

After a few minutes, I knew it was okay to finish eating my lunch. I believe God had just wanted to remind me how it feels to have an appetite and not be able to satisfy it—how it feels to have the food right under my nose, be able to smell it, but not be able to eat it.

I returned to the kitchen, reheated my food, finished my lunch, and began to think about what had just taken place. What was the meaning of all of this? God had obviously wanted my attention to be on the hungry people around the world, but it was clear that there was more to understand. After a few days of praying and waiting on God, He began to reveal to me that this was how I had been treating my spirit before Robert's illness. In years past, my spirit had been hungry, and although there was food right under my nose, I wasn't consuming it. I had been trying to satisfy my appetite with worldly things. My spirit wasn't getting the nourishment it so badly needed.

God's Word contains power and nourishment for our spirits—but we aren't even tapping into what He has provided us. Have you ever experienced going without food for a long period of time? One year, when I was in a youth group, I participated in a fast to raise money for the hungry. We fasted for twenty-four hours while we stayed together at my church. During the fast, we were provided one-fourth cup of orange juice several times during this twenty-four hour period, which represented the minimal amount of nourishment that so many receive around the world each day. What I found most interesting about the fast was that after a certain amount of time without food, my appetite faded. I didn't feel hungry any longer, although I certainly felt very weak, tired, and frustrated. Keep in mind that this was only for twenty-four hours. I have absolutely no comprehension of how it feels to go days without food like so many are forced to do.

I believe this experience is a good example of what sometimes happens to our spirits. We deny our spirits nourishment as we fill our lives with worldly things. We do not recognize that our appetites are for God as our spirits grow weaker. Within a short period of time, our appetites dull, our feelings and emotions grow stronger, and our fleshly desires overtake us. We become unhappy, frustrated, angry, unsatisfied, and weak as our spirits struggle to survive. We continually turn to additional worldly things to comfort and sustain us, and we become all the more unhappy, tired, unsatisfied, and weak.

Before long, we find ourselves drifting so far from God that we forget how wonderful He is and how much He loves us. We forget how amazing it is to spend time with Him and experience His presence. We forget how satisfying it is to experience the peace and rest that only He can provide. We have very little joy, and we can't understand why we are unsatisfied.

God has supplied us with the finest foods—and they are right under our noses. We witness others who have great relationships with Jesus. They are filled with joy and peace—so much so that we can actually smell the "fragrance of Christ" (2 Corinthians 2:15) on them. We get a small taste of Jesus now and then, but we leave feeling frustrated and unsatisfied.

In years past, I didn't understand that God's Word could actually be consumed—not by chewing up pieces of the Bible and swallowing them, but by actually praying God's living Word verbally. As God allows me to feed upon His holy Word and it passes through my mouth and penetrates my heart, my spirit is nourished in an extraordinary and powerful way.

As I think back to my lunch that day, if I hadn't eaten the hamburger, it would have been wasted and just thrown away. As we consume God's

Word, the Holy Spirit will show us things that are unique, special, and just for us at this particular time. Our lack of understanding causes us to miss opportunities that God has for us. These missed opportunities are being wasted, and we miss the chance to not only be blessed, but also witness God's glory being revealed in our everyday lives.

God has a plan for everyone's life—but that plan requires every believer's spirit to be well hydrated and nourished. God's holy words and promises are our defense—food and water for our "good fight of faith" (1 Timothy 6:12).

I recently stumbled across these words from Deuteronomy 8:3 in a devotional that I was flipping through one morning: "So He humbled you, allowed you to hunger, and fed you with manna which you did not know nor did your fathers know, that He might make you know that man shall not live by bread alone; but man lives by every *word* that proceeds from the mouth of the LORD" (NKJV).

As I read these words, I couldn't help but feel that God was using them to speak to me directly. Robert and I have definitely been humbled by aplastic anemia, and we have most certainly experienced a higher level of hunger for the Lord. God *did* literally feed us the months that Robert was unable to work, and interestingly enough, one of our parents *did* comment that she had never witnessed such unique provision from the Lord. Most importantly, we do now know unequivocally that "man shall not live by bread alone, but by every word that proceeds from the mouth of the Lord".

We don't have to wait for the rainy seasons to experience God in a mighty way. Even in the drought, our thirst can be quenched, our leaves can be lush and green, and our lives can flourish and bear God-produced "fruit" (John 15:8). This is best worded in Psalm 1:1–3: "Blessed is the man Who walks not in the counsel of the ungodly, Nor stands in the path of sinners, Nor sits in the seat of the scornful; But his delight *is* in the law of the LORD, and in His law he meditates day and night. He shall be like a tree Planted by the rivers of water, That brings forth its fruit in its season, Whose leaf also shall not wither And whatever he does shall prosper" (NKJV).

God has recently given me the opportunity to watch other believers' lives flood with His Word. As they have humbly replaced their words with God's living words, I have personally witnessed many of my friends' and family members' lives transform as God's living water revived them.

God promises us in Isaiah 57:15, "I dwell in the high and holy place, but with him also who is of a thoroughly penitent and humble spirit, to revive the spirit of the humble and to revive the heart of the thoroughly penitent [bruised with sorrow for sin]" (AMP).

"God also says: 'When the time's ripe, I answer you. When victory's due, I help you. I form you and use you to reconnect the people with me, to put the land in order, to resettle families on the ruined properties. I tell prisoners, 'Come on out. You're free!' and those huddled in fear, 'It's all right. It's safe now.' There'll be foodstands along all the roads, picnics on all the hills—Nobody hungry, nobody thirsty, shade from the sun, shelter from the wind for the Compassionate One guides them, takes them to the best springs. I'll make all my mountains into roads, turn them into a superhighway" (Isaiah 49:8-11, *The Message*).

"Shout for joy, you heavens; rejoice, you earth; burst into song, you mountains! For the LORD comforts his people and will have compassion on his afflicted ones" (Isaiah 49:13, NIV).

From the beginning, I thought this book was mainly about sharing my family's experiences and journey with you. I naturally wanted to help and encourage you to experience God and enjoy His blessings. However, I have since gained a much deeper understanding. It is now obvious that this book was actually an important part of the journey itself. As you can see, there was much more God had to teach me, and there was more to this book than I realized.

As God so graciously reminded me during my lunch that day, I have done none of this on my own. In John 15:5 Jesus says, "Apart from Me you can do nothing" (NIV). It is apparent that God led me to pray and put His words in my "mouth" (Isaiah 51:16) from the very beginning.

With that being said, will you take the words of Jesus from John 15:5 into account and once again seriously consider that it was, in fact, God's idea for you to read this book? Would you now believe that God truly does want your attention?

If you struggle or find it difficult to relate this verse to your own life, then please consider mine. As I mentioned in the beginning, I am neither a teacher nor a pastor. I have no formal education or credentials to be writing this book. In fact, I find it somewhat challenging to creatively write in a greeting card. I am convinced that God has a sense of humor. This work is certainly beyond my natural abilities. It truly is our Almighty God who enables and empowers us to do all things.

Although our lives are certainly blessed and enriched through our experiences with the Lord, it is apparent that this isn't about you and me. It is most importantly about the "glory of God" (Philippians 2:11).

Previously, we were assured of this incredible promise from Psalm 50:15: "Call upon Me in the day of trouble; I will deliver you and *you shall glorify Me*" (NKJV). Notice the last words of this verse. As we believers experience God's provision, His glory is revealed through our lives. We get the incredible honor of making much of Jesus! You and I actually get to participate in making Jesus famous! In my opinion, life just doesn't get any better than that.

I have been very humbled by this opportunity, and I want to thank you for traveling alongside me as God has allowed us to witness a glimpse of His glory. We have just tapped into the many mysteries of God's Word, and I look forward to the endless adventures that await.

I encourage you to not wait until the rainy seasons to *call upon* the Lord with childlike faith flooding your life with His Word. Don't settle for a life of just getting by, allowing your spirit to look like my cherry tree did a couple of years ago. Don't stop at the gate of righteousness. "Enter His gates with thanksgiving and His courts with praise" (Psalm 100:4), feasting on His Word, and "take, appropriate, and drink the water of Life" (Revelation 22:17, AMP). "Rejoice and be glad and *give Him glory!*" (Revelation 19:7, NIV)

> "'As for me,' God says, 'this is My covenant with them: My Spirit that I've placed upon you and the words that I've given you to speak, they're not going to leave your mouths nor the mouths of your children nor the mouths of your grandchildren. You will keep repeating these words and won't ever stop.' God's orders" (Isaiah 59:21, *The Message*).

Chance has not brought this ill to me;
It's God's own hand, so let it be,
For He sees what I cannot see.
There is a purpose for each pain,
And He one day will make it plain
That earthly loss is heavenly gain.
Like as a piece of tapestry
Viewed from the back appears to be
Only threads tangled hopelessly;
But in the front a picture fair
Rewards the worker for his care,
Proving his skill and patience rare.
You are the Workman, I the frame.
Lord, for the glory of Your Name,
Perfect Your image on the same.

(L. B. Cowman, *Streams in the Desert*)

Acknowledgments

Special recognition for this work is extended to my pastor and church family. It has been amazing to witness God use you to participate in bringing this book to fruition. I would like to express special thanks to Pastor Jeff and my sister in Christ, Tina, for your advice, support, and encouragement along the way. I also want to thank Mandy for your special contribution, and I extend my appreciation to my small group for your support and encouragement.

I am very grateful to my husband and daughter for your contributions to this book, and for the patience, constant love, and support you have shown me through the countless hours sacrificed for this work.

We are indebted to our entire family and to all of our friends. Words cannot express our appreciation for the compassion, support, prayers, and gifts that have been showered upon us as we have traveled through this journey with aplastic anemia over the past several years. The glory of God has shown brightly through your obedience. We are truly blessed to have you in our lives.

I am especially thankful for my parents and two older brothers. I am eternally grateful for the loving environment I was provided throughout my childhood and the godly examples set before me.

To all platelet and blood donors—you are our heroes! Thank you for your sacrifice and service to my family and the countless individuals whose lives have been and are being saved by your donations. Special thanks go to the platelet donors. The many extra hours you sacrifice are commendable. May God bless you all.

Most importantly, we thank God for using our hands to create this work. We praise You, Lord, for Your faithfulness and Your powerful promises. Thank you for the deliverance You will bring as Your holy Word is spoken through the prayers of Your people.

I want to personally thank you for your purchase. Ninety percent of the royalties from this book will be given to God; most of which will be used to help feed the hungry and build schools and orphanages in Africa and other impoverished countries in the name of Jesus Christ. As I write this, a school on the outskirts of Kenya by the name of Sandota Education Centre is presently under construction.

"If you spend yourselves in behalf of the hungry

and satisfy the needs of the oppressed,

then your light will rise in the darkness,

and your night will become like the noonday.

The LORD will guide you always;

he will satisfy your needs in a sun-scorched land

and will strengthen your frame. You will be like a well-watered

garden, like a spring whose waters never fail.

Your people will rebuild the ancient ruins

and will raise up the age-old foundations;

you will be called Repairer of Broken Walls,

Restorer of Streets with Dwellings."

Isaiah 58:10–12 (NIV)

Thank you for your support. For more information, go to *www.childlikefaith.org.*

God bless you,

Tessa Gaines

Promises

Psalm 138:2 (AMP)

"I will worship toward Your holy temple and praise Your name for Your loving-kindness and for Your truth and faithfulness; for You have exalted above all else Your name and Your Word and You have magnified Your Word above all Your name!"

Psalm 29:4 (NIV)

"The voice of the LORD is powerful; the voice of the LORD is majestic."

Joel 2:11 (AMP)

"And the Lord utters His voice before His army, for His host is very great, and [they are] strong and powerful who execute [God's] Word."

Psalm 103:20 (AMP)

"Bless (affectionately, gratefully praise) the Lord, you His angels, you mighty ones who do His commandments, hearkening to the voice of His Word."

Jeremiah 1:9 (AMP)

"And the Lord said to me, Behold, I have put My words in your mouth."

Jeremiah 1:12 (AMP)
"I am alert and active, watching over My word to perform it."

Psalm 119:89 (NIV)
"Your Word, O LORD, is eternal; it stands firm in the heavens."

Psalm 119:114 (AMP)
"You are my hiding place and my shield; I hope in your Word."

Mark 9:23 (NIV)
"'If you can?' said Jesus. 'Everything is possible for him who believes.'"

Luke 1:37 (AMP)
"For with God nothing is ever impossible and no word from God shall be without power or impossible of fulfillment."

Romans 4:16 (NIV)
"Therefore, the promise comes by faith, so that it may be by grace and may be guaranteed to all Abraham's offspring—not only to those who are of the law but also to those who are of the faith of Abraham. He is the father of us all."

Acts 3:25 (NIV)
"And you are heirs of the prophets and of the covenant God made with your fathers. He said to Abraham, 'Through your offspring all peoples on earth will be blessed.'"

Isaiah 55:3 (NIV)
"Give ear and come to me; hear me, that your soul may live. I will make an everlasting covenant with you, my faithful love promised to David."

Hebrews 7:22 (NIV)
"Because of this oath, Jesus has become the guarantee of a better covenant."

2 Peter 1:4 (NIV)
"Through these he has given us his very great and precious promises, so that through them you may participate in the divine nature."

Matthew 17:20 (NIV)
"I tell you the truth, if you have faith as small as a mustard seed, you can say to this mountain, 'Move from here to there' and it will move. Nothing will be impossible for you."

Joshua 23:14 (NIV)
"You know with all your heart and soul that not one of all the good promises the LORD your God gave you has failed. Every promise has been fulfilled; not one has failed."

John 14:12–17 (NIV)
"I tell you the truth, anyone who has faith in me will do what I have been doing. He will do even greater things than these, because I am going to the Father. And I will do whatever you ask in my name, so that the Son may bring glory to the Father. You may ask me for anything in my name, and I will do it. "If you love me, you will obey what I command. And I will ask the Father, and he will give you another Counselor to be with you forever— the Spirit of truth. The world cannot accept him, because it neither sees him nor knows him. But you know him, for he lives with you and will be in you."

John 15:7 (NIV)
"If you remain in Me and My words remain in you, ask whatever you wish, and it will be given you."

Psalm 37:5 (NIV)
"Commit your way to the LORD; trust in him and He will do this."

Jeremiah 32:27 (NIV)
"I am the LORD, the God of all mankind. Is anything too hard for Me?"

Isaiah 55:11 (NIV)
"So is my Word that goes out from My mouth: It will not return to Me empty, but will accomplish what I desire and achieve the purpose for which I sent it."

Hebrews 4:16 (AMP)
"Let us then fearlessly and confidently and boldly draw near to the throne of grace (the throne of God's unmerited favor to us sinners), that we may receive mercy [for our failures] and find grace to help in good time for every need [appropriate help and well-timed help, coming just when we need it]."

Isaiah 53:4–5 (NIV)
"Surely he took up our infirmities and carried our sorrows, yet we considered him stricken by God, smitten by him, and afflicted. But he was pierced for our transgressions, he was crushed for our iniquities; the punishment that brought us peace was upon him, and by his wounds we are healed."

Psalm 119:154 (AMP)
"Plead my cause and redeem me; revive me and give life according to your Word."

Psalm 30:2 (NKJV)
"O LORD my God, I cried out to You, and You healed me."

Psalm 103:3 (NIV)
"The Lord forgives all your sins and heals all your diseases."

Psalm 107:20 (AMP)
"He sends forth His Word and heals them and rescues them from the pit and destruction."

Psalm 118:17 (AMP)
"I shall not die but live, and shall declare the works and recount the illustrious acts of the Lord."

Isaiah 58:8 (AMP)
"Then shall your light break forth like the morning, and your healing (your restoration and the power of a new life) shall spring forth speedily."

Jeremiah 17:14 (AMP)
"Heal me, O Lord, and I shall be healed; save me, and I shall be saved, for You are my praise."

1 Peter 2:24 (NIV)
"He himself bore our sins in his body on the tree, so that we might die to sins and live for righteousness; by his wounds you have been healed."

Psalm 119:49 (NIV)
"Remember your Word to your servant, for you have given me hope."

1 Thessalonians 5:24 (NIV)
"The one who calls you is faithful and he will do it."

Romans 4:18-21 (NIV)
"Against all hope, Abraham in hope believed and so became the father of many nations, just as it had been said to him, 'So shall your offspring be.' Without weakening in his faith, he faced the fact that his body was as good as dead—since he was about a hundred years old—and that Sarah's womb was also dead. Yet he did not waver through unbelief regarding the promise of God, but was strengthened in his faith and gave glory to God, being fully persuaded that God had power to do what he had promised."

Acts 27:25 (NIV)
"So keep up your courage, men, for I have faith in God that it will happen just as He told me."

Psalm 91:16 (AMP)
"With long life will I satisfy him and show him My salvation."

1 Chronicles 17:23–24 (NIV)
"And now, LORD, let the promise you have made concerning your servant and his house be established forever. Do as you promised, so that it will be established and that your name will be great forever."

Psalm 119:116 (AMP)
"Uphold me according to your promise, that I may live; and let me not be put to shame in my hope!"

Revelations 12:11 (NIV)
"They overcame him by the blood of the Lamb and by the word of their testimony."

Ephesians 6:10 (NIV)
"Finally, be strong in the Lord and in his mighty power."

Psalm 91:9–11 (AMP)
"Because you have made the Lord your refuge, and the Most High your dwelling place, there shall no evil befall you, nor any plague or calamity come near your tent. For He will give His angels [especial] charge over you to accompany and defend and preserve you in all your ways [of obedience and service]."

Mark 11:22 (AMP)
"And Jesus, replying, said to them, Have faith in God [constantly]."

Hebrews 13:20–21 (NIV)
"May the God of peace, who through the blood of the eternal covenant brought back from the dead our Lord Jesus, that great Shepherd of the sheep, equip you with everything good for doing His will, and may He work in us what is pleasing to Him, through Jesus Christ, to whom be glory for ever and ever. Amen."

Small Group Discussion Guide

Chapter 1—Growing Pains

Icebreaker: The author asked you to relate her experience with God's love and the baby girl to your life. What child came to mind when you were asked to relate this story to your life?

Can you relate to what is said about God's love? How do you think God feels about you?

Can you look back and think of a circumstance in your life that was not enjoyable, but was later revealed to be something good or positive for you? Share these experiences.

Reflect on the battle or battles you are presently fighting in your life. Do you believe that you are fighting the battles, or are you allowing God to fight the battles for you?

Discuss steps or actions of faith that must be taken to allow God to fight your battles.

Chapter 2—Don't Fall for It

Icebreaker: Have you seen *Sherlock Holmes?* Do you agree with the parallels?

Could you be living a life deceived by the enemy's illusions? Discuss the illusions that exist in different aspects of your life.

What are these illusions producing in your life? Are they controlling your actions? How?

Share times when you have experienced the spirit of fear so strongly that you were left feeling powerless.

Have there been times in your life that you have fallen into the trap of fear? Did fear directly reflect in your disobedience to God? What plan of action can you take to stop the deceit?

Are you living a life filled with anxiety, fear, and stress? Could this be a sign that you are not putting your confidence in God?

Do you believe that fear can diminish your faith? Does it steal your confidence in God?

Chapter 3—No One is Good

Icebreaker: Do you agree that no one is good on their own?

Can you relate to the explanation of positive and negative thoughts? Do you agree with the explanation?

Do you believe obeying God is as simple as recognizing, following, and acting upon the positive thoughts in your mind?

Can you think of an experience in your life when you were worried and upset, but later found that everything turned out all right? Do you believe the negative thoughts stole your peace?

Do you believe that the enemy manipulates you? Could you be giving the enemy power through the fear in your life? Discuss how you can take back this power.

What action can you take to stop this from occurring in your life? Read Romans 8:15 and discuss the difference between fear and faith.

Chapter 4—Born to Fly

Icebreaker: Do you believe reading this book was your idea? Could the fact that you thought it was your idea be a type of an illusion?

Have you ever experienced God speaking to you? If not, do you agree that the positive thoughts are actually from God and that is how He leads you?

Are you angry with God? Do you blame Him for something that happened in your life? Could the bad circumstance have been brought into your life by a bad choice?

If not, can you relate to the story of the baby bird being pushed out of the nest? Could it have been an experience that grew and developed a stronger relationship with God? Share examples.

Chapter 5—I Shall Not be Moved

Icebreaker: How can you use God's Word as your defense?

Can you think of a time that God's Word has come to your rescue?

Do you believe that Jesus speaking God's Word to overcome the temptations of the enemy has been given to you as an example? Do you believe that God wants you to deal with temptations in this matter?

Discuss times that the enemy has used illusions to tempt you. How can you use God's Word to overcome those temptations?

Do you believe that being familiar with the covenant God made with Abraham is important to us today? How?

Chapter 6—Lay Down Beside Him

Icebreaker: Do you trust and rest in the fact that God will do what is best for you through the good and the bad circumstances of your life?

Can you recall a time in your life when you used praise and worship as a weapon of defense against the enemy? What was the outcome? Discuss areas in your life where you could use this type of defense against the enemy.

In what circumstances can you allow God to act as your umpire? How could this change your perspective?

Have you ever been on a boat in the water and caught in a bad storm? Discuss what it was like and what you felt.

Are you presently experiencing a storm in your life? Discuss what it would look like to lay down in the boat in the water and rest beside Jesus in your storm.

Chapter 7—Don't Lose Your Flavor

Icebreaker: Do you ever get caught up in the actions of others instead of focusing on your own reaction to others?

Share a time in your life that your obedience caused you unfavorable consequences. Also share times in your life that you experienced favorable consequences from your obedience.

How can you use love in your life as a weapon against the enemy?

Do you believe that your pride often convinces you that your opinion about others holds weight? Have you ever became angry and counteracted your obedience by your actions? How?

Do you believe that with God's help, you can overcome your feelings and control your actions? How can others see God's love and light through your actions? Discuss.

Chapter 8—He Goes Before You

Icebreaker: Do you believe that God goes before you?

Do you believe that God has already prepared for your challenging circumstances in the future? Do you worry about your future? If so, do your actions show God that you trust Him with your future?

Have you ever experienced the Holy Spirit preparing you for a challenging experience ahead of time? Discuss a time that God clearly went before you.

Did this experience build your faith? How?

Read Luke 22:31-32. Can you relate these verses to your own life? Discuss the comforting fact that Jesus prays for you ahead of time and prays that your faith will not fail when you face the storms and temptations of life.

Chapter 9—Walk By Faith

Icebreaker: What percentage of your life do you suppose you live by faith and not by sight?

Do you think most people believe that they are in control of their lives? If so, do you think this is just an illusion? Discuss why.

Have you ever experienced a time in your life when you clearly saw that God changed your plans for a specific reason? After recognizing God's hand in that circumstance, did the experience strengthen your faith?

Are you currently facing a difficult situation in your life that you can see no logical way out of? Have you presented your petition to the Lord?

Search for a promise from God's Word that you can use as evidence for your petition.

Chapter 10—Become Childlike

Icebreaker: What are some characteristics of children that you admire? What can you do to display more childlike faith?

How is a child's perspective different than an adult's?

As a child of God, do you trust Him to care for you? Do your actions and attitude prove to God that you look to Him and trust Him completely? Discuss what that would look like.

Do you believe that God places us purposely in uncomfortable situations at times in our lives to help others? Share your experiences.

Do you allow your concerns for the future to dictate your present happiness?

After bringing a concern to the Lord, are you confident that He will take care of it? How does your life reflect that confidence?

Chapter 11—A Sling and a Stone

Icebreaker: Do you believe that every word that comes out of your mouth affects your life? How?

As you turn to God and wait on Him to move in your life, do you allow your circumstances or what people say to weaken your faith? Why? Discuss how to prevent this.

Do you believe that God's Word contains power?

Discuss whether the promises in the Bible were intended only for the time that they were recorded or are they for us today.

Do you believe that God is faithful to keep His promises and fulfill His Word? Discuss why.

Do you believe that your faith will grow as you speak and pray God's promises out loud and hear His words?

Discuss how you could use the Bible as a book of prayers.

Chapter 12—Pleading the Promises

Icebreaker: Do you agree that speaking and praying God's Word out loud is an action of faith? Discuss why doing this requires a higher degree of faith than just reading it quietly to yourself?

Read Luke 1:5-45 and discuss how we limit God and His promises. Discuss verse 37.

Do you believe that speaking and praying God's promises will make a difference in your life?

Have you ever heard someone say they don't believe everything that they read in the Bible because it was written by man? Discuss why people say that about the Bible and not about history books?

Do you know anyone who believes that Jesus died on the cross for them but doesn't believe the other stories in the Bible? Is it possible to believe some of the Bible and not all of it?

Do you believe that the enemy is responsible for the negative thoughts that tempt us to doubt?

Discuss guilt and how it can affect your life.

Chapter 13—Enjoy the Warm Water

Icebreaker: What is your favorite time of day to spend with God?

Do you make spending time with God as big of a priority as your physical cleanliness?

Discuss creative ways to spend time with God.

Do you believe it is important to renew and cleanse your spirit? Discuss which is more important—cleansing your spirit or your physical body?

Do you believe that God watches you and loves you unconditionally? What would it take for you to accept that He loves and forgives you and wants to spend time with you?

Discuss how the condition of the heart can play an important role in a believer's prayer life. Discuss what it means to harbor sin in your heart.

Chapter 14—Beware of the Camel

Icebreaker: Do you find it hard to turn over control of your life to God?

Why do you believe some people get angry at God over circumstances in their lives? Are you ever tempted to be angry with God? Share times you have been upset with Him.

In this chapter, we read about the boundaries that the gate appears to represent. What kind of boundaries has God set for you in your life that at first seemed oppressive or negative but turned out to be a gift?

Are you presently comfortable with your relationship with God? Do you believe that stepping out in faith is comfortable? Discuss how being comfortable might possibly be a warning sign that the enemy is deceiving you.

Have you noticed roadblocks that seem intentionally placed to get you off the path that God has planned for you? Are you acting on your fear or your faith? Discuss how you can overcome your fears.

Is there an area of your life where God might be waiting for you to take the first step of faith? Are you "sitting at the gate"?

Chapter 15—Honey from the Rock

Icebreaker: Have you experienced struggles in your life that have taught you more about God? Share your experiences.

What would it look like to trust God and accept and embrace the unfavorable circumstances in your life—even when you are not getting your way?

Do you spend time focusing on God and praising Him instead of focusing on the bad circumstances in your life? Discuss how that might change your circumstances.

In this chapter, we read about the honey or testimony that is only produced by God. Do you have testimonies that you need to share with others?

Do you believe that your testimony can nourish other believers? Has fear kept you from sharing your testimony with others? Discuss steps you can take to overcome this fear.

Chapter 16—Our Deliverer

Icebreaker: Has God ever delivered you out of a bad circumstance? Were you aware that it was Him? Share your experiences.

Discuss how to recognize the enemy and his games in your everyday life? (For example: negative thoughts) Discuss ways that fear affects our lives and keeps us from stepping out in faith and obedience.

Do you recognize God's Word as ammunition for your defense against the enemy? Discuss how to put your faith into action and use God's Word as your defense.

Share times that God has delivered you *in* your circumstances. Did the time of waiting on God teach you anything about Him?

Chapter 17—Sing a New Song

Icebreaker: We all want to prove to God that we believe and trust Him. Discuss examples of actions that prove to God that we believe and trust Him.

In 1 Peter 5:5–6, we are told, "God opposes the proud but gives grace to the humble. Humble yourselves, therefore, under God's mighty hand, that he may lift you up in due time" (NIV). What actions can you take to humble yourself before God?

In this chapter, we are told that when we align our lives with God's will through His Word, we are actually surrendering ourselves to God. Are there other ways to surrender ourselves to God? Discuss.

What actions do you take to acknowledge and worship God?

What acts of obedience and faith in God have required you to step out of your comfort zone? Share these experiences.

How do you believe incorporating God's Word into your prayer life will affect your relationship with God?

Endnotes

Chapter 1

1. L. B. Cowman, *Streams in the Desert: 366 Daily Devotional Readings.* (Grand Rapids, MI: Zondervan, 1997), 178.
2. L. B. Cowman, *Streams in the Desert: 366 Daily Devotional Readings.* (Grand Rapids, MI: Zondervan, 1997), 178.

Chapter 2

1. Peter Davies and William Morris, Ed., *The American Heritage Dictionary of the English Language.* (New York: Dell Publishing Co., Inc., 1980), 352, 244.
2. Henry T. Blackaby and Richard Blackaby, *Experiencing God Day-By-Day Devotional.* (Nashville, TN: Broadman & Holman Publishers, 1998), 127.
3. Henry T. Blackaby and Richard Blackaby, *Experiencing God Day-By-Day Devotional.* (Nashville, TN: Broadman & Holman Publishers, 1998), 123.

Chapter 3

1. Peter Davies and William Morris, Ed., *The American Heritage Dictionary of the English Language.* (New York: Dell Publishing Co., Inc., 1980), 550.

2. Peter Davies and William Morris, Ed., *The American Heritage Dictionary of the English Language.* (New York: Dell Publishing Co., Inc., 1980), 471.

Chapter 6

1. "Forensic Anthropology Center," University of Tennessee College of Arts and Science, accessed November 15, 2010, http://web.utk.edu/~fac/faq.html.
2. "Official American Football." *Wikipedia.com,* accessed November 9, 2010, http://en.wikipedia.org/wiki/Official_(American football).
3. Peter Davies and William Morris, Ed., *The American Heritage Dictionary of the English Language.* (New York: Dell Publishing Co., Inc., 1980), 748.

Chapter 8

1. Henry T. Blackaby and Richard Blackaby, *Experiencing God Day-By-Day Devotional.* (Nashville, TN: Broadman & Holman Publishers, 1998), 86.

Chapter 9

1. Joel Osteen, *Your Best Life Now: 7 Steps to Living at Your Full Potential.* (New York,: Warner Faith, 2004), 281.
2. L. B. Cowman, *Streams in the Desert: 366 Daily Devotional Readings.* (Grand Rapids, MI: Zondervan, 1997), 189–190.
3. L. B. Cowman, *Streams in the Desert: 366 Daily Devotional Readings.* (Grand Rapids, MI: Zondervan, 1997), 78–79.

Chapter 10

1. L. B. Cowman, *Streams in the Desert: 366 Daily Devotional Readings.* (Grand Rapids, MI: Zondervan, 1997), 79–80.
2. L. B. Cowman, *Streams in the Desert: 366 Daily Devotional Readings.* (Grand Rapids, MI: Zondervan, 1997), 177.

Chapter 11

1. Jim Cymbala and Dean Merrill, *Fresh Faith: What Happens When Real Faith Ignites God's People.* (Grand Rapids, MI: Zondervan, 2003), 116.
2. Jim Cymbala and Dean Merrill, *Fresh Faith: What Happens When Real Faith Ignites God's People.* (Grand Rapids, MI: Zondervan, 2003), 115.
3. Peter Davies and William Morris, Ed., *The American Heritage Dictionary of the English Language.* (New York: Dell Publishing Co., Inc., 1980), 257.
4. Jim Cymbala and Dean Merrill, *Fresh Faith: What Happens When Real Faith Ignites God's People.* (Grand Rapids, MI: Zondervan, 2003), 116.

Chapter 12

1. Joel Osteen, *Your Best Life Now: 7 Steps to Living at Your Full Potential.* (New York,: Warner Faith, 2004), 127.
2. L. B. Cowman, *Streams in the Desert: 366 Daily Devotional Readings.* (Grand Rapids, MI: Zondervan, 1997), 165.
3. "Plead the Promises of God." Leadership U. Bible Prayer Fellowship, accessed October, 2010, http://www.leaderu.com/orgs/bpf/pathways/plead.html#.

Chapter 13

1. Jim Cymbala and Dean Merrill, *Fresh Faith: What Happens When Real Faith Ignites God's People.* (Grand Rapids, MI: Zondervan, 2003), 116.
2. Henry T. Blackaby and Richard Blackaby, *Experiencing God Day-By-Day Devotional.* (Nashville, TN: Broadman & Holman Publishers, 1998), 294.
3. Jim Cymbala, *Breakthrough Prayer: The Power of Connecting with the Heart of God.* (Grand Rapids, MI: Zondervan, 2003), 84.
4. L. B. Cowman, *Streams in the Desert: 366 Daily Devotional Readings.* (Grand Rapids, MI: Zondervan, 1997), 90.

Chapter 16

1. "The Names of God, Lesson #3, JEHOVAH—Rapha—The Lord That Healeth Thee Exodus 15:25–26," *Freegrace.net,* accessed November 18, 2010, http://www.freegrace.net/dfbooks/dfnamesgodbk/names3.htm.

Chapter 17

1. "Unabridged Based on the Random House Dictionary." *Dictionary.com*, accessed November 18, 2010, http://dictionary.reference.com/browse/confess.

Ending Poem selected from *Streams in the Desert: 366 Daily Devotional Readings* by L. B. Cowman.

Made in the USA
Charleston, SC
30 June 2016